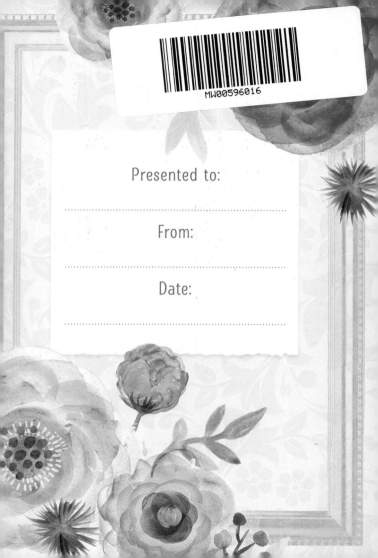

Presented to:

....

From:

....

Date:

....

© 2016 by Barbour Publishing, Inc.

Print ISBN 978-1-64352-968-4

Compiled and edited by Emily Biggers.

Several prayers are taken from *Prayers & Promises for Women* by Toni Sortor, *Prayers & Promises for Mothers* by Rachel Quillin and Nancy Farrier, and *365 Power Prayers for Women Perpetual Calendar*, published by Barbour Publishing, Inc.

Scripture quotations marked NASB are taken from the New American Standard Bible, (NASB 1995) © 1960, 1962, 1963, 1968, 1971, 1972, 1973, 1975, 1977, 1995 by The Lockman Foundation. Used by permission.

Scripture quotations marked NIV are taken from the HOLY BIBLE, NEW INTERNATIONAL VERSION®. NIV®. Copyright © 1973, 1978, 1984, 2011 by Biblica, Inc.™ Used by permission. All rights reserved worldwide.

Scripture quotations marked NLT are taken from *Holy Bible*, New Living Translation. Copyright © 1996, 2015. Used by permission of Tyndale House Publishers, Incorporated, Carol Stream, Illinois 60188. All rights reserved.

Published by Barbour Publishing, Inc., 1810 Barbour Drive, Uhrichsville, Ohio 44683, www.barbourbooks.com

Our mission is to inspire the world with the life-changing message of the Bible.

Member of the
Evangelical Christian
Publishers Association

Printed in China.

Everyday Prayers

for Women

*365 Devotional Prayers
for Your Heart*

BARBOUR
PUBLISHING

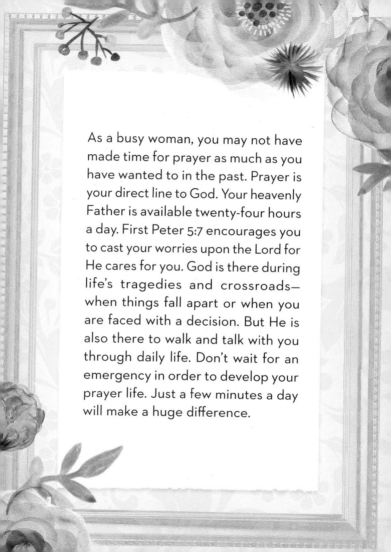

As a busy woman, you may not have made time for prayer as much as you have wanted to in the past. Prayer is your direct line to God. Your heavenly Father is available twenty-four hours a day. First Peter 5:7 encourages you to cast your worries upon the Lord for He cares for you. God is there during life's tragedies and crossroads—when things fall apart or when you are faced with a decision. But He is also there to walk and talk with you through daily life. Don't wait for an emergency in order to develop your prayer life. Just a few minutes a day will make a huge difference.

Day 1

The Peacekeeper

Lord, help me be the peacekeeper, never the one who stirs up more anger. Help me be an example to my whole family and to my friends and coworkers. You offer peace to me that the world cannot give. Help others to see that peace in me and long for it themselves, I pray. May others come to know You by seeing Jesus in me. Amen.

Great peace have those who love your law, and nothing can make them stumble.

PSALM 119:165 NIV

Day 2

Patience

Father, raising obedient, loving children requires me to show gentleness and patience, not threats or harshness. I pray that You will teach me how to soften each correction with the same love I receive from You. Help me to remember that my children may need some second chances. How thankful I am that You allow me a "do-over" from time to time! I want to be gracious yet consistent in my discipline. Give me wisdom, I pray. Amen.

Day 3

Strength to Forgive

Lord, give me the strength to forgive others so You will forgive me my own trespasses. When someone offends me, remind me of the great grace You have poured out upon me so that I may be gracious as well. In Jesus' name I pray, amen.

"Give us today our daily bread.
And forgive us our debts, as we also
have forgiven our debtors."

MATTHEW 6:11–12 NIV

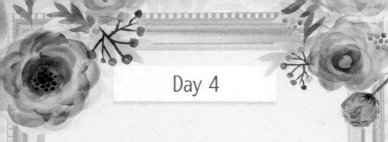

Day 4

Give Love

- -

Lord, help me not to be quick to judge or oppose love between others. Let me give love time to do its work. I may never see the result I want, but I am sure it is in Your hands. Amen.

Love is patient, love is kind. It does not envy, it does not boast, it is not proud. It does not dishonor others, it is not self-seeking, it is not easily angered, it keeps no record of wrongs. Love does not delight in evil but rejoices with the truth. It always protects, always trusts, always hopes, always perseveres. Love never fails.

1 CORINTHIANS 13:4–8 NIV

Day 5

Have Mercy on Me

Merciful God, You have forgiven me in the past and I ask You to show mercy yet again. You are a gracious God, and I am so thankful for Your open arms and for second chances. I love You, Lord. Amen.

Have mercy on me, my God, have mercy on me, for in you I take refuge. I will take refuge in the shadow of your wings.

PSALM 57:1 NIV

Day 6

Thank You!

Father, thank You for all You have given me, for all You have taught me, and for all the good times still to come. I do not have to worry about the future because I am Your daughter and You have good plans for me. You have promised never to leave me or forsake me. Thank You for Your promises, Lord. They bring such peace to my life. Amen.

She is clothed with strength and dignity;
she can laugh at the days to come.

PROVERBS 31:25 NIV

Day 7

Purpose Revealed

Heavenly Father, I pray that You will transform my mind and show me Your will for my life. When Your purpose is revealed to me, Father, help me to accept my responsibility and do Your will. Amen.

Do not conform to the pattern of this world, but be transformed by the renewing of your mind. Then you will be able to test and approve what God's will is—his good, pleasing and perfect will.

ROMANS 12:2 NIV

Day 8

God's Power Can Overcome

- -

Father, it often seems that might makes right and I stand no chance, but I know Your power can overcome whatever evil men might plan. When I am in despair, fill me with faith in Your justice. In the end, You will prevail. Remind me that while I will experience trials in this life, I am more than a conqueror through Christ Jesus, my Savior. Amen.

Day 9

Fill Me with Faith

I often feel that I lack faith, Lord, that You must be speaking promises for someone else— someone more faithful and deserving of them. Show me the error of this thinking. Amen.

He replied, "Because you have so little faith. Truly I tell you, if you have faith as small as a mustard seed, you can say to this mountain, 'Move from here to there,' and it will move. Nothing will be impossible for you."

MATTHEW 17:20 NIV

Day 10

My Fortress

Dear heavenly Father, You are a mighty tower, my fortress, a refuge I can always run to. You protect Your own. In times of trouble, I am comforted to know that You are always on my side. Thank You for this assurance, mighty God. Amen.

You are my strength, I watch for you;
you, God, are my fortress, my God
on whom I can rely.

PSALM 59:9–10 NIV

Day 11

Wise with Finances

Thank You, Lord, for the abundant life You have blessed me with. I may not always have a lot financially, but I am so blessed and happy in Christ. Help me to be wise with what money I have and to use it in a way that pleases You. Amen.

"To those who use well what they are given, even more will be given, and they will have an abundance. But from those who do nothing, even what little they have will be taken away."

MATTHEW 25:29 NLT

Day 12

Keep Me from Temptation

Lord, I am human and often tempted. I want to honor You with my life, and yet I find myself straying. Be with me when I am tempted and show me the true joys of self-control. Make me a daughter who represents her heavenly Father well in the world. I ask these things in Jesus' name, amen.

No temptation has overtaken you except what is common to mankind. And God is faithful; he will not let you be tempted beyond what you can bear. But when you are tempted, he will also provide a way out so that you can endure it.

1 CORINTHIANS 10:13 NIV

Day 13

Trust

- -

Lord, I thank You for Your guidance and protection day after day. Although I never know what the day will bring, You have a plan for my life and I choose to trust in You. Amen.

*Trust in the LORD with all your heart
and lean not on your own understanding;
in all your ways submit to him, and he
will make your paths straight.*

PROVERBS 3:5–6 NIV

Day 14

Thank You for Motherhood

Thank You, Lord, that in Your perfect plan You've seen fit to give me beautiful children whom I probably don't deserve. Thank You for allowing me to be a mother. That is truly a gift from You. Help me not to take this gift for granted. Make me a godly mother. In Jesus' name I pray, amen.

Her children arise and call her blessed; her husband also, and he praises her.

PROVERBS 31:28 NIV

Day 15

My Rock

Lord, You alone are my rock. You are my fortress. You deliver me from evil, and whenever there is trouble in my life, I take refuge in You. You are my shield, my salvation, and my stronghold (Psalm 18:2). You are all I need. Amen.

Turn your ear to me,
come quickly to my rescue;
be my rock of refuge,
a strong fortress to save me.

PSALM 31:2 NIV

Never Alone

Father, when troubles come, I never have to face them alone. Thank You for always being with me as my refuge and strength. When all else fails, I put my trust in You and am never disappointed. You have promised me in Your Word that nothing can separate me from You. Amen.

My Father, who has given them to me, is greater than all; no one can snatch them out of my Father's hand.

JOHN 10:29 NIV

Day 17

The Victor

- -

Precious Father, on my own, I am bound to fail. Now that I have put my trust in You, I cannot fail, for You are always the Victor, and this knowledge makes me strong where once I was weak. Amen.

"The LORD your God is with you,
the Mighty Warrior who saves.
He will take great delight in you;
in his love he will no longer rebuke you,
but will rejoice over you with singing."

ZEPHANIAH 3:17 NIV

Day 18

A Virtuous Woman

Lord, I want to help bring others to You, to be judged a virtuous woman for Your sake, not for any glory that might come to me. Use me as You see fit, because any work You give me to do is an honor. Amen.

Who can find a virtuous and capable wife?
She is more precious than rubies.
Her husband can trust her, and she will
greatly enrich his life. She brings him good,
not harm, all the days of her life.

PROVERBS 31:10–12 NLT

Make My Home
a Blessing

- -

Lord, I want my house to be Your house—a house of prayer, a place of comfort and peace, a refuge to those in need. Just as I give of my money and time, please help me to be a good steward of this structure I call "home." May my home be a blessing to all who pass through its door, whether they are here for a short visit or a longer stay. I want to honor You as I use my home for Kingdom work. Amen.

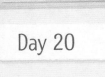

Answer Me, O Lord

Do not let the floodwaters engulf me or the depths swallow me up or the pit close its mouth over me. Answer me, LORD, out of the goodness of your love; in your great mercy turn to me. Do not hide your face from your servant; answer me quickly, for I am in trouble. Come near and rescue me; deliver me because of my foes.

PSALM 69:15–18 NIV

Day 21

My Time

Help me invest my time in more worthy pursuits, Lord, ones that will provide lasting satisfaction. I'm not sure what You will ask of me, but I am willing to try anything You recommend and give any resulting praise to You. Amen.

Work willingly at whatever you do, as though you were working for the Lord rather than for people. Remember that the Lord will give you an inheritance as your reward, and that the Master you are serving is Christ.

COLOSSIANS 3:23–24 NLT

Day 22

Much-Needed Courage

Father, I need the courage of a soldier going into battle. Each day I am on the front lines of a spiritual battle. Satan would love to see me fail. Help me. Go before me into battle. Give me supernatural courage that can only come from You. Amen.

"So be strong and courageous!
Do not be afraid and do not panic
before them. For the LORD your God
will personally go ahead of you. He will
neither fail you nor abandon you."

DEUTERONOMY 31:6 NLT

Day 23

Grant Me Strength

Lord, I would prefer to live a life of peace, but when I must fight for those I love, I pray You will give me the strength to do so. When I must stand up for what is right, I pray for the right words and actions. Amen.

That is why, for Christ's sake, I delight in weaknesses, in insults, in hardships, in persecutions, in difficulties. For when I am weak, then I am strong.

2 CORINTHIANS 12:10 NIV

Day 24

Consolation and Comfort

There are wars and rumors of wars, Father. I ask for Your comfort for all the wives and mothers who sit and wait, regardless of where their loved ones are serving in the military forces. Thank You for Your consolation and comfort. Amen.

"Peace I leave with you; my peace I give you. I do not give to you as the world gives. Do not let your hearts be troubled and do not be afraid."

JOHN 14:27 NIV

Do Not Be Afraid

Mighty God, I do not have to fight the battle that is before me. I must simply take my position and trust in You to deliver me. This is not my battle but Yours. I will not be afraid or discouraged. I will face this fight, and You will be with me (2 Chronicles 20:17). Amen.

"Do not be afraid! Don't be discouraged by this mighty army, for the battle is not yours, but God's."

2 CHRONICLES 20:15 NLT

A Better Future

Father God, the joy has gone out of my life. I need Your reassurance that You will never give me a burden without helping me bear it. Be my strong hope for a better future. You know the plans You have for me, even though they are not clear to me today. They are plans to give me hope, not to harm me (Jeremiah 29:11). I will trust You to lead me one day at a time. Replace my anxiety with joy, I pray. Amen.

Day 27

Wisdom and Guidance

Jesus, my Wonderful Counselor, I ask for Your wisdom and guidance. Instruct me in the ways that I should go. I trust that You will guide me so I may serve You all the days of my life. Amen.

For to us a child is born, to us a son is given, and the government will be on his shoulders. And he will be called Wonderful Counselor, Mighty God, Everlasting Father, Prince of Peace.

ISAIAH 9:6 NIV

Instruct My Children

Lord, help me teach my children about You, about Your great promises, and about the peace that I pray will be their inheritance. Give me opportunities to speak into the lives of other children as well, Father. So many of our children's friends do not know You as the one true God. I pray that through our family, others will come to know You. In Jesus' name I pray, amen.

Day 29

In Time of Loss

I know that death comes to us all, Lord, but sometimes I feel I cannot give up a loved one. I know that heaven is a better place, but in my humanity, I am so limited. I want to keep my loved ones here with me. In times of loss, send me Your comfort and peace, I pray. Help me to remember that grief is the price I must pay for love and that it is well worth it. Amen.

Day 30

A Prayer from Beth Moore's Heart

Father God, I ask You to lead me when I'm blinded by ways I have not known, along unfamiliar paths please guide me. Lord, turn the darkness into light before me and make the rough places smooth. I pray these are the things You will do; I know You will not forsake me (Isaiah 42:16).

—from *Praying God's Word: Breaking Free from Spiritual Strongholds*

Day 31

For All Things. . .

- -

Thank You, precious heavenly Father, for giving us all the things we need for life and godliness. You are Jehovah-Jireh, the Great Provider. Amen.

And because of his glory and excellence, he has given us great and precious promises. These are the promises that enable you to share his divine nature and escape the world's corruption caused by human desires.

2 PETER 1:4 NLT

Day 32

Sing Praises

I praise You, Father, from the mountaintops—
when things go well. It is easy there! But in
those times when things go wrong, help me to
praise You still. Give me the faith to praise You
from the valleys of my life. You are sovereign,
and all of Your ways are perfect. Amen.

I will give thanks to you, LORD, with all my
heart; I will tell of all your wonderful deeds.
I will be glad and rejoice in you; I will sing
the praises of your name, O Most High.

PSALM 9:1–2 NIV

Day 33

True Forgiveness

Heavenly Father, show me the way to true forgiveness. Help me to forgive as I have been forgiven. It is not always easy, but it is always Your will for me in Christ Jesus. Amen.

"For if you forgive other people when they sin against you, your heavenly Father will also forgive you. But if you do not forgive others their sins, your Father will not forgive your sins."

MATTHEW 6:14–15 NIV

Day 34

Blessing Others

Lord Jesus, draw my family close to You. Fill our home with Your presence and our lives with Your love. In turn, help each one of us to realize the importance of blessing others. Amen.

"But who am I, and who are my people, that we should be able to give as generously as this? Everything comes from you, and we have given you only what comes from your hand."

1 CHRONICLES 29:14 NIV

Day 35

Guidance for Children

Dear heavenly Father, please give me the wisdom I need to properly advise my children. Help me teach them to seek guidance from Your Word and communion with the Holy Spirit. Help me to be an example as I live out my life before them. In Jesus' name I pray, amen.

I have hidden your word in my heart
that I might not sin against you.

PSALM 119:11 NIV

Day 36

My Light

- -

Jesus, You are the Light of the world. If I follow
You, I will never walk in darkness. I will have
the light of life (John 8:12). May I always walk
in the light. Amen.

*You, LORD, are my lamp; the LORD turns
my darkness into light. With your
help I can advance against a troop;
with my God I can scale a wall.*

2 SAMUEL 22:29–30 NIV

Day 37

Just Right

Thank You, Lord, for being so faithful. Thank You for Your compassion—which is just the right amount to get me through the day. Give me each day my daily bread, I pray. Amen.

Keep falsehood and lies far from me;
give me neither poverty nor riches,
but give me only my daily bread.

PROVERBS 30:8 NIV

"Give us each day our daily bread."

LUKE 11:3 NIV

True Contentment

Lord, show me how to be a godly woman, how to have true contentment that comes from service to You. Help me to reinforce in my home the need to be satisfied with doing Your will. So many times I want to add to this. I think we need a bigger house, the newest fashions, or a car like the neighbors have. Help us to be satisfied in You. Amen.

Day 39

Today!

Lord, help me to rejoice in the time I have
with my family today. I don't want to dwell on
what might happen in the future; I want to
relish this chance to nurture and cherish the
blessings You've given me. Help me to live in
the moment. Amen.

*"Therefore do not worry about tomorrow,
for tomorrow will worry about itself. Each
day has enough trouble of its own."*

MATTHEW 6:34 NIV

Day 40

God Meets My Needs

Father, help me realize that my wants are temporary and of little importance. Let me lean against You, Lord, relaxed in the knowledge that You will care for me. You know my needs far better than I do. Amen.

For the LORD God is a sun and shield;
the LORD bestows favor and honor;
no good thing does he withhold
from those whose walk is blameless.

PSALM 84:11 NIV

Day 41

The Shepherd

Dear Jesus, You are my Good Shepherd. You
have sacrificed Your very life for me. I know
Your voice (John 10:4). I will follow it all the days
of my life. If I go astray and listen to another
voice, I pray that You will lead me back to the
right path. I love You, Savior. Amen.

*Save your people and bless your
inheritance; be their shepherd
and carry them forever.*

PSALM 28:9 NIV

Day 42

The Example

You are an example for me in all things, Lord Jesus. You were a servant leader when You walked on this earth. You noticed those who went unnoticed by others. You were a friend of sinners. You gave second chances. You were gracious. You met needs. You gave until it hurt. May I be a little bit more like You each day. I may be the only Jesus some will ever see. May my life lead others to You, I pray. Amen.

Day 43

Godly Woman

Lord, help me to be a godly woman. May others notice my loving spirit rather than the name brands that I wear. May my beauty come from within. May friends and even acquaintances be blessed for time spent in my presence. May my deeds reflect the great love and grace that You have shown me. In Jesus' name I pray, amen.

I also want the women to dress modestly, with decency and propriety, adorning themselves, not with elaborate hairstyles or gold or pearls or expensive clothes, but with good deeds, appropriate for women who profess to worship God.

1 TIMOTHY 2:9–11 NIV

Day 44

The Answers

Father, I know my understanding is weak. But when I am in need of guidance, the first place I turn to is Your Word. Help me to search diligently, for I know the answers I need are there. May Your Word be hidden in my heart so that I may not sin against You (Psalm 119:11). Amen.

Jesus answered, "It is written: 'Man shall not live on bread alone, but on every word that comes from the mouth of God.'"

MATTHEW 4:4 NIV

With Love

Lord, I want to love the way You do. I want to be strong, to lovingly discipline my children so they will grow to be pleasing to You. I want to speak life into my sisters' lives with love. I want to show love to those who are less fortunate than I am by giving generously. I want to love even when it is difficult. Give me a loving heart, I pray. Amen.

Day 46

Rejoice!

God, I rejoice in You. I find a hiding place in You. When the world threatens me, I claim that I am secure as a daughter of the King. I know that Your protection is always surrounding me. I will rejoice in You all the days of my life. Amen.

But let all who take refuge in you be glad;
let them ever sing for joy. Spread your
protection over them, that those who love
your name may rejoice in you. Surely, Lord,
you bless the righteous; you surround them
with your favor as with a shield.

Psalm 5:11–12 niv

Day 47

Don't Worry

----

*"Look at the lilies and how they grow.
They don't work or make their clothing,
yet Solomon in all his glory was not dressed
as beautifully as they are. And if God cares
so wonderfully for flowers that are here
today and thrown into the fire tomorrow,
he will certainly care for you. Why do you
have so little faith? And don't be concerned
about what to eat and what to drink. Don't
worry about such things. These things
dominate the thoughts of unbelievers all
over the world, but your Father already
knows your needs. Seek the Kingdom of
God above all else, and he will give
you everything you need."*

LUKE 12:27–31 NLT

Understanding

Lord, help me to be understanding with my children, to encourage rather than discourage. I want to take their hands and walk with them, as You've taken time to walk with me. I want to build them up and never tear them down. May they find in me one who sees the best in them, one who hears them and truly listens, and above all—may they know that they are dearly loved. I pray these things in Jesus' name, amen.

Day 49

"Forever"

Forever, Lord—what encouragement is in that word. We have all eternity to spend with You in heaven. Thank You for this indescribable gift. Thank You for being the Alpha and the Omega, the first and the last. Amen.

"I am the Alpha and the Omega—the beginning and the end," says the Lord God. "I am the one who is, who always was, and who is still to come—the Almighty One."

REVELATION 1:8 NLT

Day 50

God's Children

Lord, I'm grateful that I can show my children where to turn in times of trouble. They don't have to try to do it all themselves, because we are all Your children. Amen.

But to all who believed him
and accepted him, he gave the
right to become children of God.

JOHN 1:12 NLT

See how very much our Father loves us,
for he calls us his children, and that is what
we are! But the people who belong to this
world don't recognize that we are God's
children because they don't know him.

1 JOHN 3:1 NLT

God Is Great

When I was young, God, I recited a simple prayer at mealtimes. It went like this: *God is great. God is good. Let us thank Him for our food.* I remember outgrowing that prayer, realizing that I should speak my heart to You rather than just words I had memorized. And yet, there was a great truth in that little prayer. You are great. May I never grow too old to recognize Your greatness. Amen.

Your ways, God, are holy.
What god is as great as our God?
You are the God who performs miracles;
you display your power among the peoples.

PSALM 77:13–14 NIV

Day 52

Let the Light Shine

Lord, if there's one thing I need, it is trust-worthy guidance. In darkness or light, on fair days or foul, I trust that the light of Your Word will bring me safely home. I am so thankful that I can trust in the darkness what I have seen in the light. Amen.

The light shines in the darkness, and the darkness can never extinguish it.

JOHN 1:5 NLT

Day 53

God's Will

Lord, help me to live according to Your guidelines and show my children that Your plan is best as they strive to live for You. I want them to see in their mother a woman who is more concerned with pleasing You than pleasing men. I want them to learn to trust You day by day. I cannot teach them these things on my own. I need Your help to raise godly children. Amen.

Day 54

Advice

Lord, show me my errors and teach me the proper way to take advice. Help me always to seek godly counsel. I can be so stubborn, but I know that I need to receive advice at times in order to make good decisions. Grant me a more open mind and heart. Put in my path women to mentor me, women who have attained godly wisdom over the years. Such women are rare treasures. Amen.

The wise in heart are called discerning,
and gracious words promote instruction.
PROVERBS 16:21 NIV

For Good

Father, give me Your peace and an understanding that all things work together for good when I follow Your will. Amen.

Commit to the LORD whatever you do, and he will establish your plans. The LORD works out everything to its proper end.

PROVERBS 16:3–4 NIV

And we know that in all things God works for the good of those who love him, who have been called according to his purpose.

ROMANS 8:28 NIV

Day 56

Bless Me, O Lord

Father God, I need Your blessing over my life. As I rise and go about my day, please bless the work of my hands. Please make me the kind of woman I should be. Make me a blessing to all those who cross my path whether at home or in the workplace. I want to be blessed and to be a blessing. Amen.

"I have obeyed the LORD my God and have done everything you commanded me. Now look down from your holy dwelling place in heaven and bless your people."

DEUTERONOMY 26:14–15 NLT

Like You, Jesus

Lord Jesus, help me to follow Your example because I have a family following mine. You are kind, gentle, forgiving, not easily angered, and always looking out for my best interest. Help me as I strive to be like You. I have little eyes watching me. I have little ears listening to me. I have little attitudes being molded by what they observe. You said that faith, hope, and love were all important, but You pointed out love as the greatest of all. Help me to love with my whole heart. Amen.

Day 58

Right Paths

Father, Your Word contains the best parenting instruction and advice I could ever possess. Give me the wisdom to weigh everything else I read against what the Bible says. Thank You for leading me in right paths. Amen.

He refreshes my soul. He guides me along the right paths for his name's sake.

PSALM 23:3 NIV

The righteousness of the blameless makes their paths straight, but the wicked are brought down by their own wickedness.

PROVERBS 11:5 NIV

Day 59

Called to Be Godly

- -

Lord, I'm called to live a godly life—not by
childishness, but by Your grace and virtue.
Thank You for Your provision. Amen.

Finally, all of you, be like-minded,
be sympathetic, love one another,
be compassionate and humble. Do not
repay evil with evil or insult with insult.
On the contrary, repay evil with blessing,
because to this you were called so
that you may inherit a blessing.

1 PETER 3:8–9 NIV

A Prayer from Mother Teresa's Heart

Dear Jesus, help us to spread Your fragrance everywhere we go. Penetrate and possess our whole being so utterly that our lives may only be a radiance of Yours. Let them look up and see no longer us, but only Jesus. Stay with us and then we shall begin to shine as You shine, so to shine as to be light to others. The light, O Jesus, will be all from You. It will be You shining on others through us. Let us thus praise You in the way you love best by shining on those around us. Let us preach You without preaching, not by words, but by our example.

Day 61

Be Glad

God, I do not know how many days I have left
on this earth, but I commit each one to You.
You are my joy and my salvation. Even if I grow
old and cannot do as much as I once could, I
will praise You still. You will be my joy even in
old age. Amen.

Teach us to number our days,
that we may gain a heart of wisdom....
Satisfy us in the morning with your
unfailing love, that we may sing for
joy and be glad all our days.
PSALM 90:12, 14 NIV

Day 62

Keep Me Faithful

Lord, when times are hard and I become discouraged, be with me. Keep me a faithful teacher of the Way for the sake of my children and all those to come. May the next generation see You in me, I pray. Amen.

We will not hide them from their descendants; we will tell the next generation the praiseworthy deeds of the LORD, his power, and the wonders he has done.

PSALM 78:4 NIV

Day 63

God's Representative

- -

Lord, I know I am Your representative here on earth and should give no one the opportunity to reject You because of my actions. When I am within seconds of being a bad example, send me Your peace. Amen.

And let us consider how we may spur one another on toward love and good deeds, not giving up meeting together, as some are in the habit of doing, but encouraging one another—and all the more as you see the Day approaching.

HEBREWS 10:24–25 NIV

Day 64

I Will Praise You

Just as You rescued Your servant David, You reach down and rescue me. I will praise You for Your wonderful creation, for Your steadfast love, and for being the one true God. Please, Father, let me never tire of giving You the praise that You are due. Amen.

"I will praise you, LORD, among the nations;
I will sing the praises of your name."

2 SAMUEL 22:50 NIV

Day 65

Sufficient Grace

Father, when I am a poor example to someone I meet, grant me forgiveness. Grant those I offend the wisdom to understand that no one is free of sin, but Your grace is sufficient. Amen.

But he said to me, "My grace is sufficient for you, for my power is made perfect in weakness." Therefore I will boast all the more gladly about my weaknesses, so that Christ's power may rest on me.

2 CORINTHIANS 12:9 NIV

Day 66

Faithful Companion

Be with all women living alone, Lord. Be especially near to their hearts, I pray. Whether they are single, divorced, or widowed, be their faithful Companion and Guide as they strive to build a life based on Your principles. Amen.

For your Maker is your husband—the LORD Almighty is his name—the Holy One of Israel is your Redeemer; he is called the God of all the earth.

ISAIAH 54:5 NIV

Day 67

Attitude Adjustment

Lord, I need an attitude adjustment that can
only come from You. Let me be a cheerful
worker. Resolve my conflicted feelings and
give me Your peace. Amen.

*Create in me a pure heart, O God,
and renew a steadfast spirit within me.
Do not cast me from your presence
or take your Holy Spirit from me.
Restore to me the joy of your salvation
and grant me a willing spirit, to sustain me.*

PSALM 51:10–12 NIV

Day 68

Help Me to Live by Your Word

Lord, help me study Your Word and grow in knowledge of You in order to attain godliness. Then I can help others around me to understand how to live godly lives. Help me to place a high priority on reading and applying Your holy Word. Amen.

All Scripture is God-breathed and is useful for teaching, rebuking, correcting and training in righteousness.

2 TIMOTHY 3:16 NIV

Day 69

Before Me

I pray that You will go before me, God. I cannot see more than one step at a time, but You see the path that You have set me on. You see the future, and You know the ways in which I should go. Go before me, walk beside me, and stay near to me, I pray. I believe that I can do all things because You are with me. Amen.

I keep my eyes always on the LORD. With him at my right hand, I will not be shaken.

PSALM 16:8 NIV·

A Constant Reminder

As I read Your Word, it is a constant reminder of Your love for me. It also reminds me of how much You love my husband and my children and that You have their best interests at heart. Amen.

And hope does not put us to shame,
because God's love has been poured
out into our hearts through the Holy Spirit,
who has been given to us.

ROMANS 5:5 NIV

Heart Cleansing

Lord, let me know when I am wrong. That way I can come to You for cleansing and an opportunity to make things right. Thank You for the truth in Your Word, even though sometimes the truth hurts. Help me to grow as a result of correction, I pray. Amen.

If you reject discipline, you only harm yourself; but if you listen to correction, you grow in understanding.

PROVERBS 15:32 NLT

Day 72

Teach Me to Relax

Heavenly Father, I find it hard to find time to relax. Thank You for making me to lie down even when I don't want to. Thank You for leading me beside quiet waters when I need the solace. Amen.

The LORD is my shepherd; I have all that I need. He lets me rest in green meadows; he leads me beside peaceful streams. He renews my strength.

PSALM 23:1–3 NLT

Day 73

No Matter What

- -

Lord, remove the fears that bind me so that I can be happy in the knowledge that You are there to comfort me—no matter what else is happening. Amen.

Not that I was ever in need, for I have learned how to be content with whatever I have. I know how to live on almost nothing or with everything. I have learned the secret of living in every situation, whether it is with a full stomach or empty, with plenty or little.

PHILIPPIANS 4:11–12 NLT

Day 74

I Will Fear No Evil

I have no reason to fear, God. I may walk through some tough times. Eventually, I will face the valley of the shadow of death. But I will not face it alone. You are always with me, protecting me and guiding me. You are my comfort and my shield. I am so thankful that You are my Good Shepherd. Amen.

Even though I walk
through the darkest valley,
I will fear no evil,
for you are with me;
your rod and your staff,
they comfort me.

PSALM 23:4 NIV

Day 75

Make Me an Instrument

Lord, I want to be instrumental in helping my family establish a close walk with You. Direct me daily to renew my commitment to follow in Your steps. Thank You for being the example I need. Amen.

Let us therefore make every effort to do what leads to peace and to mutual edification.

ROMANS 14:19 NIV

Day 76

Slowing Down

Father, I need rest—rest from my schedule, rest from the demands of my family, rest from "doing" to a place of simply "being." Lead me to that place. Calm my mind and my emotions so I can slow down enough to find real rest. Amen.

"Take my yoke upon you and learn from me, for I am gentle and humble in heart, and you will find rest for your souls. For my yoke is easy and my burden is light."

MATTHEW 11:29–30 NIV

Day 77

Give and It Will Be Given unto You

Lord, You told me to give and that if I do, it shall be given to me. Your generosity is unmatched, and Your blessings are always wonderful. Thank You! Amen.

"Give, and it will be given to you. A good measure, pressed down, shaken together and running over, will be poured into your lap. For with the measure you use, it will be measured to you."

LUKE 6:38 NIV

Day 78

The Best

- -

Lord, I need Your gentle wisdom for every area of life. I'm so thankful that what You offer is the best. Amen.

"You fathers—if your children ask for a fish, do you give them a snake instead? Or if they ask for an egg, do you give them a scorpion? Of course not! So if you sinful people know how to give good gifts to your children, how much more will your heavenly Father give the Holy Spirit to those who ask him."

LUKE 11:11–13 NLT

Into Glory

Thank You, Father, for the calm assurance that one day I will be with You in heaven. Jesus is preparing a place for me there even now. I am doubly blessed because I have been given this abundant life on earth and eternal life with You in glory. Amen.

You guide me with your counsel,
and afterward you will take me into glory.

PSALM 73:24 NIV

Day 80

To Be Gentle

Father, You gave me my children to cherish, and that includes being gentle with them. I do treasure them, Lord, so help me to impart Your gentleness to them. Amen.

A gentle answer turns away wrath, but a harsh word stirs up anger.

PROVERBS 15:1 NIV

You should clothe yourselves instead with the beauty that comes from within, the unfading beauty of a gentle and quiet spirit, which is so precious to God.

1 PETER 3:4 NLT

Day 81

Joy and Strength

Thank You, God, for Your Word. It instructs me on how to live. It brings joy to my days and gives me strength when I am weak. You are my joy. You are my strength. Amen.

The LORD is my strength and shield.
I trust him with all my heart.
He helps me, and my heart is filled with joy.
I burst out in songs of thanksgiving.
PSALM 28:7 NLT

Day 82

How to Trust

Lord, I'm ashamed to admit that sometimes I have a hard time taking You at Your Word. Please show me how to trust You more, even when my mind can't grasp it and my heart can't accept it. Help me never to trust more in man or in man-made things than I trust in my heavenly Father. Amen.

"Do not put your trust in idols or make metal images of gods for yourselves. I am the LORD your God."

LEVITICUS 19:4 NLT

Day 83

Listen Up

Father, I get discouraged when I don't know which way to go. Remind me that You are right behind me, telling me which way to turn. Help me to be quiet and listen for Your guidance. Sometimes it comes through Your still, small voice. I cannot hear Your instruction or heed Your directions if I am not focused and listening. Amen.

Good and upright is the LORD;
therefore he instructs sinners in his ways.
PSALM 25:8 NIV

Day 84

Not Shaken

I am not like those who do not know You, Lord. Disaster shakes them. Even if I walk through the valley of the shadow of death, I will not be shaken. My God goes with me. You are my hope, and I find my rest and calm assurance in You. Amen.

Yes, my soul, find rest in God;
my hope comes from him.
Truly he is my rock and my salvation;
he is my fortress, I will not be shaken.

PSALM 62:5–6 NIV

Day 85

The Good Shepherd

Father, Your guidance is trustworthy. You are our Good Shepherd. You lead us to places of rest when we need them. I need that rest. Thank You for Your leading. Amen.

Then, because so many people were coming and going that they did not even have a chance to eat, he said to them, "Come with me by yourselves to a quiet place and get some rest."

MARK 6:31 NIV

Day 86

Be Joyful

There's no mistaking, Lord. You've made it clear that I'm to be joyful in each and every task. The next time I'm tempted to complain about the mounds of work, remind me to turn my murmuring into praise. Amen.

Though the fig tree does not bud
and there are no grapes on the vines,
though the olive crop fails
and the fields produce no food,
though there are no sheep in the pen
and no cattle in the stalls,
yet I will rejoice in the LORD,
I will be joyful in God my Savior.

HABAKKUK 3:17–18 NIV

Reflecting Glory

Gracious Father, I thank You for the work I have. You made work, and it is part of every man and woman's life. May I do my work, whether in the home or beyond its walls, in a way that is pleasing to You and that reflects Your glory. Amen.

The LORD God took the man and put him in the Garden of Eden to work it and take care of it.

GENESIS 2:15 NIV

Priorities

Father, praising You and rejoicing in You must be high on my priority list. Proclaiming Your love to others must never be lacking in my life. Thank You that I am able to rejoice in You! Amen.

Jesus replied: "'Love the Lord your God with all your heart and with all your soul and with all your mind.'"

MATTHEW 22:37 NIV

Day 89

A Close Walk

- -

Father God, joy fills my life when my son asks me to read a book to him and then he chooses one about You. I pray that this is the beginning of a close walk that he will eventually have with You. Amen.

Start children off on the way they should go, and even when they are old they will not turn from it.

PROVERBS 22:6 NIV

A Prayer from Elisabeth Elliot's Heart

We are women, and my plea is, "Let me be a woman, holy through and through, asking for nothing but what God wants to give me, receiving with both hands and with all my heart whatever that is."

Day 91

Teach Me Your Way

Lord, I wish that I could say my heart is undivided. I am pulled in so many different directions lately. I want to meet the needs of so many—my husband and children, my parents, my coworkers and neighbors. . .slow my pace, Father. Take my face in Your hands. Speak peace over me and remind me that if I have a divided heart, I will miss out on so many blessings that You have for me. Amen.

Teach me your way, LORD,
that I may rely on your faithfulness;
give me an undivided heart,
that I may fear your name.
PSALM 86:11 NIV

Day 92

Always Ready

Father, I don't know how You will use my life, but I have faith in Your promises and am always ready to do Your will. Help me to recognize that life is a journey, not a destination. There is not just one big purpose for my life. Every day You have opportunities for me to be about Kingdom work. Help me to notice that person You would have me encourage or share the Gospel with. Help me to use my resources and abilities to honor You each day. That is Your will for me, and I want to be about Your business. Amen.

Day 93

A Friend

I love my children, Lord. I thank You for them, but sometimes I need another person to talk to who understands what I'm going through. Help me find a friend—someone who needs the kind of companionship I do. I need a friend, and I would like to be a good friend to another as well. Amen.

A friend loves at all times, and a brother is born for a time of adversity.

PROVERBS 17:17 NIV

Doubt

Forgive me, Lord, for those times when I've doubted Your love. I know that even when doors close in my life, You are preparing a way for me—the right way. Sometimes I get so frustrated, feeling as if nothing ever works out for me. I know that is a lie from Satan. Let me rest in You and know that You are there. Thank You for being with me, Father. Thank You for the good plans You have for my future. Amen.

An Ambassador

I am Your ambassador, Lord, and every day I try to show Your love to those who do not know You. I pray that I will have the right words today, Lord. There are times when actions speak even louder than words. Guide and direct me as I live in this world without being truly part of it. Heaven is my home. When I get there, I want to recognize many faces of people whom You allowed me to share Jesus with. Amen.

Day 96

Hear My Voice

----

*I call with all my heart; answer me, LORD,
and I will obey your decrees. I call out to
you; save me and I will keep your statutes.
I rise before dawn and cry for help; I have
put my hope in your word. My eyes stay open
through the watches of the night, that I may
meditate on your promises. Hear my voice
in accordance with your love; preserve my
life, LORD, according to your laws. Those who
devise wicked schemes are near, but they
are far from your law. Yet you are near,
LORD, and all your commands are true.*

PSALM 119:145–152 NIV

Day 97

Teach Me to Discipline

Father, I want my children to know what I expect of them and then obey. Give me guidance to establish the right discipline system. I need strength in that area, Lord. I have started many times, but I get lazy and become inconsistent. I want to honor You by bringing up disciplined children. Amen.

No discipline seems pleasant at the time,
but painful. Later on, however, it produces
a harvest of righteousness and peace for
those who have been trained by it.

HEBREWS 12:11 NIV

Day 98

Patience by Example

God, You tell us in scripture that we should clothe ourselves with patience. Still my complaining heart, O Lord. Fill me with rejoicing. Help me to slow down and to take time for others. I want to be an example of patience to those around me. Give me strength for the task. Amen.

*Therefore, as God's chosen people,
holy and dearly loved, clothe yourselves
with compassion, kindness, humility,
gentleness and patience.*

COLOSSIANS 3:12 NIV

Day 99

My Children

Father, I know You blessed me abundantly in the children You have given me. Help me not to flaunt them or to take any credit that belongs to You. Help me to remember that You have entrusted them into my care. Give me wisdom as I care for them, discipline them, and love them. Help me to love them well. I want them to become young men and women who serve the one true God. Amen.

Day 100

Steadfast and Dedicated

Father, my daily problems come and go; yet if I remain steadfast and dedicated, doing the work You have given me to do, I am confident that my reward awaits me in heaven. Give me the endurance that I need to press on in the faith. Thank You, Lord. Amen.

"Rejoice and be glad, because great is your reward in heaven, for in the same way they persecuted the prophets who were before you."

MATTHEW 5:12 NIV

Day 101

Remember the Miracles

----

*"I will remember the deeds of the LORD;
yes, I will remember your miracles of long
ago. I will consider all your works
and meditate on all your mighty deeds."
Your ways, God, are holy. What god is as
great as our God? You are the God who
performs miracles; you display your power
among the peoples. With your mighty arm
you redeemed your people, the descendants
of Jacob and Joseph. . . . You led your people
like a flock by the hand of Moses and Aaron.*

PSALM 77:11–15, 20 NIV

Day 102

Inner Strength

Lord, I can see Your inner power at work in my children as they grow in You. Your Spirit inside us is a life-changing power that will always be available to us wherever we are. Thank You for this wonderful gift. Amen.

David was greatly distressed because the men were talking of stoning him; each one was bitter in spirit because of his sons and daughters. But David found strength in the LORD his God.

1 SAMUEL 30:6 NIV

Day 103

Cleansed by the Blood

I've made mistakes, Lord. But someday You will present me faultless, cleansed by Your blood. The evidence of Your power to lift me up and make me whole fills me with exceeding joy. I will praise You forever and forever. Amen.

The more you grow like this, the more productive and useful you will be in your knowledge of our Lord Jesus Christ. But those who fail to develop in this way are shortsighted or blind, forgetting that they have been cleansed from their old sins.

2 PETER 1:8–9 NLT

Take Control

I sometimes want to rely on my own power rather than Yours, Lord. I pray that I will allow You to sit in the driver's seat of my life rather than just ride along as a passenger whom I consult with now and then. I know that Your ways are higher than mine and Your thoughts are as well. I swerve all over the road. You can keep me on the straight paths. Your boundaries for me are pleasant. Please take control of my life. I love You, Lord. Amen.

Day 105

Song of Joy

- -

Put a new song in my mouth, Lord. Let my
children see me being patient and waiting
on You, no matter what difficulty I'm facing.
Help them learn the same song of joy that You
are giving me. Amen.

"There will be joy and songs of thanksgiving,
and I will multiply my people, not diminish
them; I will honor them, not despise them."

JEREMIAH 30:19 NLT

Day 106

The Lord Is with You!

God, You have been with Your children throughout the ages. Nothing has changed. You are the same yesterday, today, and tomorrow. Remind me of Your steadfast love and make me courageous enough to speak Your name and witness to others about salvation in Jesus. Amen.

"Stand still and watch the Lord's victory. He is with you, O people of Judah and Jerusalem. Do not be afraid or discouraged. Go out against them tomorrow, for the Lord is with you!"

2 Chronicles 20:17 nlt

Visible Patience and Kindness

Lord, I ask for Your help in raising my children. May Your patience and kindness be made visible through my actions. I want them to sense just a glimmer of their heavenly Father's sweet love through their mother's love. I am so imperfect, and in my humanity, I will continue to make mistakes with these precious ones. Help me to quickly turn when I do and return to Your ways. I need Your help, Father. This is not easy for me. Amen.

Day 108

Faithfulness

Father, give me faithfulness in all things large and small, so that I may be an example to my children and a blessing to my husband—and to all those near me. Amen.

She must be well respected by everyone because of the good she has done. Has she brought up her children well? Has she been kind to strangers and served other believers humbly? Has she helped those who are in trouble? Has she always been ready to do good?

1 TIMOTHY 5:10 NLT

Day 109

Completion of God's Plan

Lord, help me realize that my understanding is not necessary for the completion of Your plan. You understand everything; all I need to do is have faith. You will complete the good work You have begun in my life. Please use me in any way You so desire. Amen.

Being confident of this, that he who began a good work in you will carry it on to completion until the day of Christ Jesus.

PHILIPPIANS 1:6 NIV

Day 110

Fairness

Lord, help me not to judge, but to let You decide the fairness of matters. Give me patience—to rest in You and to wait for Your return. I need Your help to teach my children to rest in You too. Amen.

Therefore judge nothing before the appointed time; wait until the Lord comes. He will bring to light what is hidden in darkness and will expose the motives of the heart. At that time each will receive their praise from God.

1 CORINTHIANS 4:5 NIV

Day 111

Our Protector

Hear the cries of Your people, Father. Just as You did in ancient times, I pray that You will protect and deliver us. In the name of Jesus I pray, amen.

The LORD is king forever and ever! The godless nations will vanish from the land. LORD, you know the hopes of the helpless. Surely you will hear their cries and comfort them. You will bring justice to the orphans and the oppressed, so mere people can no longer terrify them.

PSALM 10:16–18 NLT

Day 112

Answered Prayer

Lord, when I see how You have interceded on my behalf, I want to fall on my face before You. My prayers have been answered in miraculous ways. In times when all I could see was darkness, You provided light and power and hope. Amen.

In the same way the Spirit also helps our weakness; for we do not know how to pray as we should, but the Spirit Himself intercedes for us with groanings too deep for words; and He who searches the hearts knows what the mind of the Spirit is, because He intercedes for the saints according to the will of God.

ROMANS 8:26–27 NASB

Day 113

Count It All Joy

Lord, You are made strong in my weaknesses. I need Your help to remember that and to teach my children that we should count it all joy when we are faced with trials and suffering. We await a wonderful eternity in heaven with You, where all of this earthly "stuff" will fade away. The things of God are all that really matter. Amen.

You suffered along with those in prison and joyfully accepted the confiscation of your property, because you knew that you yourselves had better and lasting possessions.
HEBREWS 10:34 NIV

Without Fear

- -

Lord, the next time I am faced with danger
for Your sake, let me remember that You are
faithful to reward Your people, no matter how
much I may fear. Amen.

*"And the one on whom seed was sown
on the good soil, this is the man who
hears the word and understands it; who
indeed bears fruit and brings forth, some a
hundredfold, some sixty, and some thirty."*

MATTHEW 13:23 NASB

Never Forsaken

There are times, Lord, when I feel as if You've forgotten me. How could I let those feelings of being forsaken overwhelm me? Help me to remember that the Creator of the entire universe holds me in His hands! You know the number of hairs on my head. You know me fully. You created me and You will walk with me all the days of my life. You will never leave me or forsake me. You are faithful to Your own. Amen.

Day 116

Worthy

We give praise to many people and things that are unworthy, Father. Concert halls are sold out daily so that people may sing along with every word as an artist performs. We worship fashion, money, and social status. We give praise to mere men. Remind me when I begin to stray that You are the one true God and the only One who is worthy of praise. Amen.

I called to the LORD, who is worthy of praise, and I have been saved from my enemies.

PSALM 18:3 NIV

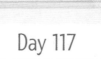

Day 117

Eternal Promise

Thank You for Your promise to preserve me if I love You, Father. I know that this is an eternal promise. What more incentive do I need to pursue a right walk with You? Keep me on the right path, Lord. Amen.

O love the LORD, all you His godly ones!
The LORD preserves the faithful
and fully recompenses the proud doer.

PSALM 31:23 NASB

Day 118

True Love

Thank You, Jesus, for Your sacrificial love for me. Thank You for the example of true love that You have provided. May I be crucified with You and allow You to reign in my heart and live through me. Amen.

I have been crucified with Christ; and it is no longer I who live, but Christ lives in me; and the life which I now live in the flesh I live by faith in the Son of God, who loved me and gave Himself up for me.

GALATIANS 2:20 NASB

Day 119

Assurance

Lord, help me to put aside my needs, to draw
my child close, and to assure him of my love
and, more importantly, of Your love. Faith in
You brings an assurance like no other available
to men. Amen.

*Let us draw near to God with a sincere heart
and with the full assurance that faith brings,
having our hearts sprinkled to cleanse us
from a guilty conscience and having our
bodies washed with pure water.*

HEBREWS 10:22 NIV

Day 120

A Servant's Heart

Father, I need a reminder that what I should be is a servant. I get so wrapped up in the need to maintain order that I forget my true job—to meet the needs of my family. Please give me a servant's heart. Help me to take time to notice the worried look in my husband's eyes and ask him about his concerns. Help me to slow down on the organization and perfectionism and truly serve my spouse and my children. Amen.

A Prayer from Anne Brontë's Heart: "Confidence"

Oppressed with sin and woe,
A burdened heart I bear,
Opposed by many a mighty foe;
But I will not despair.
With this polluted heart,
I dare to come to Thee,
Holy and mighty as Thou art,
For Thou wilt pardon me.
I need not fear my foes,
I need not yield to care;
I need not sink beneath my woes,
For Thou wilt answer prayer.
In my Redeemer's name,
I give myself to Thee;
And, all unworthy as I am,
My God will cherish me.

Day 122

Small Beauty

- -

Father, please don't let me fall into the trap of false pride. Whatever small beauty I bring into this world is only a tiny reflection of Your beauty, Your creation, Your perfection. May I add a touch of beauty to Your world today through a kind action or a generous deed. May my beauty always come from within, where You abide in my heart. Amen.

Charm is deceptive, and beauty is fleeting; but a woman who fears the LORD is to be praised.

PROVERBS 31:30 NIV

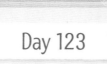

A Team

Father, teach my husband and me to work together as a team in raising our children, sharing the good times and the bad, so that neither of us should be overburdened. He has strengths that I do not possess and vice versa. Put a guard over my tongue and help me not to interrupt when he is working with our children. He is their father, and they need to hear from him. Amen.

Day 124

Comforting Opportunities

Set before me opportunities to comfort others as You comfort me. Help me to be ready to comfort a child or a friend in need, an aging parent, or even a complete stranger. We all need comfort at times. Amen.

Blessed be the God and Father
of our Lord Jesus Christ, the Father
of mercies and God of all comfort,
who comforts us in all our affliction so
that we will be able to comfort those who
are in any affliction with the comfort with
which we ourselves are comforted by God.

2 CORINTHIANS 1:3–4 NASB

Day 125

Loving Arms

- -

Father, I can't begin to count the number of times You've wrapped Your loving arms around me and calmed me in the midst of fears. You've drawn me near in times of sorrow and given me assurance when I've faced great disappointment. I am thankful for the loving arms of my everlasting God. Amen.

"The eternal God is a dwelling place, and underneath are the everlasting arms."

DEUTERONOMY 33:27 NASB

Day 126

Safe

For in the day of trouble he will keep me safe in his dwelling; he will hide me in the shelter of his sacred tent and set me high upon a rock. . . . I remain confident of this: I will see the goodness of the LORD in the land of the living. Wait for the LORD; be strong and take heart and wait for the LORD.

PSALM 27:5, 13–14 NIV

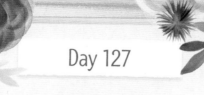

Serving

Heavenly Father, I want my children to serve You, but I know they can only do that if they have true faith in You. Help me live so that they will want this kind of faith. Help me to be an example of Christian service before them day in and day out. What they see in me will help to form the young men and women who they become. I want them to be Your faithful servants. Amen.

Teachable Moments

Lord, as a mother, I need to take advantage of the teachable moments You give me to teach my children the truths in Your Word. As we walk the aisles of the grocery store, help me to remind them that You give us the food we need to sustain our bodies. As we play at the park on a pretty day, help me take time to teach my children of Your glorious creation and praise You for the sunshine. I pray that with Your help, I'll never let an opportunity pass by. Amen.

All I Need

Father, on days when I go off on my own, draw me close to You until I calm down and begin to think clearly. Everything is under control. All I need has been provided. Thank You. Amen.

And God is able to bless you abundantly,
so that in all things at all times,
having all that you need, you will
abound in every good work.

2 CORINTHIANS 9:8 NIV

Day 130

My Hope

Lord, You are my hope in an often hopeless world. You are my hope of heaven, my hope of peace, my hope of change, purpose, and unconditional love. Fill the reservoir of my heart to overflowing with the joy that real hope brings. Amen.

For in hope we have been saved,
but hope that is seen is not hope;
for who hopes for what he already sees?
ROMANS 8:24 NASB

Day 131

All Day Long

God, my hope is in You from the moment I wake up in the morning until I lay my head down on my pillow at night. Please give me the ability to find hope even in situations that may seem hopeless. Amen.

Show me your ways, LORD, teach me your paths. Guide me in your truth and teach me, for you are God my Savior, and my hope is in you all day long.

PSALM 25:4–5 NIV

The Fruits of My Labor

When I grow old, Lord, I pray that I will see the fruits of my labor and rejoice, knowing that all my efforts were well worth the time and energy I put into them. Help me not to dread old age but help me also never to waste a day I have been given. Amen.

A gray head is a crown of glory;
it is found in the way of righteousness.

PROVERBS 16:31 NASB

Day 133

Grief

When grief comes to me, Father, I know You understand my suffering and long to comfort me. I am thankful that I do not grieve as those who have no hope. My loved ones who had accepted You are in a glorious place now! Give me a drive and a determination to pray for my lost loved ones. I do not want any of them to miss out on eternal life with You. Amen.

Brothers and sisters, we do not want you to be uninformed about those who sleep in death, so that you do not grieve like the rest of mankind, who have no hope.

1 THESSALONIANS 4:13 NIV

Parenting God's Way

Lord, You've given me plenty of instruction on parenting, and it's because You know what's best. Thank You for seeing the need to include parenting in Your Word. Help us to follow Your ways as we parent our children, I pray. Amen.

He must manage his own family well and see that his children obey him, and he must do so in a manner worthy of full respect.

1 TIMOTHY 3:4 NIV

Day 135

Small Ways

Father, there are certain children who I do not want to let into my house because of bad behavior. Show me how I can help guide them in some small way without taking over their parents' duties. Give me compassion and love for these children. Help me above all to show them love, I pray. Amen.

Above all, keep fervent in your love for one another, because love covers a multitude of sins.

1 PETER 4:8 NASB

Day 136

According to Your Love

----

*In your unfailing love preserve my life,
that I may obey the statutes of your mouth.
Your word, Lord, is eternal; it stands firm
in the heavens. Your faithfulness continues
through all generations; you established
the earth, and it endures. Your laws endure
to this day, for all things serve you. If your
law had not been my delight, I would
have perished in my affliction. I will never
forget your precepts, for by them you
have preserved my life.*

Psalm 119:88–93 niv

Day 137

Through the Eyes of a Child

- -

I know my children have a lot to teach me, Lord. Help me to be receptive of Your lessons, especially when You send them through a child. Amen.

He said to them, "Let the little children come to me, and do not hinder them, for the kingdom of God belongs to such as these. Truly I tell you, anyone who will not receive the kingdom of God like a little child will never enter it." And he took the children in his arms, placed his hands on them and blessed them.

MARK 10:14–16 NIV

Day 138

Pleasures

Lord, thank You for Your gift of physical pleasures, but teach us to use them wisely, according to Your wishes for us. Keep us faithful to our spouses and to Your laws of self-control. Help us not even to entertain the idea of adultery. Amen.

*"You have heard that it was said,
'You shall not commit adultery.' But I
tell you that anyone who looks at a
woman lustfully has already committed
adultery with her in his heart."*

MATTHEW 5:27–28 NIV

Victory

Lord, show me the path to victory every day, because sometimes I find it hard to follow. You know every turn in the road, and I will follow You in security all the days of my life. Make my paths straight as I acknowledge You as Lord of my life. I ask these things humbly in the name of Your Son, Jesus. Amen.

In all your ways acknowledge Him,
and He will make your paths straight.

PROVERBS 3:6 NASB

A Woman of Value

Thank You for the work You have given me, Father, with its opportunities to be of service to others and to You. You have made me a woman of value, and my contribution is great. Amen.

"And the very hairs on your head are all numbered. So don't be afraid; you are more valuable to God than a whole flock of sparrows."

LUKE 12:7 NLT

I Lift Up My Soul

God, so many times I rush into my day head-first without stopping to spend time in prayer. Remind me that I should lift up my day and my very soul to You before I take one step. Amen.

*Let the morning bring me
word of your unfailing love,
for I have put my trust in you.
Show me the way I should go,
for to you I entrust my life.*

PSALM 143:8 NIV

A Child of Light

Lord Jesus, You have paid for my salvation through Your death on the cross; You made me a child of light that I might guide others to You. You have made me worthy, and I thank You. Help me to shine for You in the darkness of this world. I want others to come to know You. I pray that You will use me in a mighty way. Amen.

Day 143

Obedience

Lord, I want to obey You in everything and also lead my children to obey You. Through our obedience to You, help us to reach many people for Your Kingdom. Amen.

"Whether it is favorable or unfavorable, we will obey the LORD our God, to whom we are sending you, so that it will go well with us, for we will obey the LORD our God."

JEREMIAH 42:6 NIV

Day 144

Learning to Obey

Father, I need to show my children how important obedience is by being obedient myself—to You and to others in authority over me. Thank You for assisting me in this effort. Often, I want to go my own way. Show me that Your ways are always best. Bless me with a heart that obeys You quickly and without any hesitation. Amen.

*Love the LORD your God and
keep his requirements, his decrees,
his laws and his commands always.*

DEUTERONOMY 11:1 NIV

Day 145

Unconditional Love

- -

Help me to love my children with unconditional love. Amen.

"So he returned home to his father. And while he was still a long way off, his father saw him coming. Filled with love and compassion, he ran to his son, embraced him, and kissed him. His son said to him, 'Father, I have sinned against both heaven and you, and I am no longer worthy of being called your son.' But his father said to the servants, 'Quick! Bring the finest robe in the house and put it on him. Get a ring for his finger and sandals for his feet.'"

LUKE 15:20–22 NLT

Bring Joy

I am not always joyous, Father. At times I am downright depressed. Please replace my sorrow with songs of joy. I may have to sing for a while before the joy sinks in and takes root. I love You, Father, and I want to learn to be content and joyful in all circumstances. Amen.

Bring joy to your servant, Lord,
for I put my trust in you.

PSALM 86:4 NIV

Day 147

Continual Praise

Today in anger, I said something I shouldn't have. Forgive me, Lord. Instead of speaking in anger and frustration, I want to fill my mouth with words of continual praise to You. Even when I feel angry, I do not have to sin. Set a watch over my lips, Father. Help me to take a deep breath or use another strategy in times of frustration so that I do not say things I will regret. I want to grow in this area. In Jesus' name I pray, amen.

Day 148

A Living Sacrifice

- -

Lord, make me a living sacrifice for You, that I might lead my children and others to You. Let my praises be a godly example in my home. I praise You with all that is within me. Amen.

And so, dear brothers and sisters, I plead with you to give your bodies to God because of all he has done for you. Let them be a living and holy sacrifice— the kind he will find acceptable. This is truly the way to worship him.

ROMANS 12:1 NLT

Day 149

The Gift

Lord, one of the greatest gifts You've given me is the Holy Spirit to intercede for me during prayer. Thank You, Holy Spirit, for intervening and making my requests better than I ever could. Amen.

John answered their questions by saying, "I baptize you with water; but someone is coming soon who is greater than I am—so much greater that I'm not even worthy to be his slave and untie the straps of his sandals. He will baptize you with the Holy Spirit and with fire."

LUKE 3:16 NLT

Day 150

A Beautiful Family

Thank You for blessing me with a beautiful family. I give my children back to You. I ask that You would use them for Your glory. Amen.

Hannah was in deep anguish, crying bitterly as she prayed to the Lord. And she made this vow: "O Lord of Heaven's Armies, if you will look upon my sorrow and answer my prayer and give me a son, then I will give him back to you. He will be yours for his entire lifetime, and as a sign that he has been dedicated to the Lord, his hair will never be cut."

1 Samuel 1:10–11 nlt

A Prayer from Anne Graham Lotz's Heart

(Excerpt from her poem entitled "Give Me Jesus")

He **supplies strength** to the **weary**
He **increases power** to the **faint**
He **offers escape** to the **tempted**
He **sympathizes** with the **hurting**
He **saves** the **hopeless**
He **shields** the **helpless**
He **sustains** the **homeless**
He **gives purpose** to the **aimless**
He **gives reason** to our **meaninglessness**
He **gives fulfillment** to our **emptiness**

He gives light in the darkness, comfort in the loneliness, fruit in the barrenness, future to the hopeless, life to the lifeless.

Just give me Jesus.

Day 152

With All My Heart

I want to follow You not with just part of me, but with all of my heart. Hold me close, Father. Do what it takes in my life to get me to the point of full surrender. I want to mean it when I say that I surrender all. Amen.

Teach me, LORD, the way of your decrees,
that I may follow it to the end.
Give me understanding, so that I may keep
your law and obey it with all my heart.

PSALM 119:33–34 NIV

Day 153

Redefining Greatness

Lord, help me to redefine *greatness* for my children and show them worthy examples of those who have received You. They need to know that there is a better, more glorious way to live. Amen.

Now faith is confidence in what we hope for and assurance about what we do not see. This is what the ancients were commended for. By faith we understand that the universe was formed at God's command, so that what is seen was not made out of what is visible.

HEBREWS 11:1–3 NIV

Day 154

A Merry Heart

Father, help me to get over self-doubt. Remind me that Your blessings are forever and I have nothing to fear. Give me a merry heart. Others will be drawn to me if I am joyful, but who wants to be around someone who is always complaining? Help me to be joyful so that others may know it is You who puts a smile on my face even in difficult times. Amen.

A cheerful heart is good medicine,
but a crushed spirit dries up the bones.

PROVERBS 17:22 NIV

Provision

Lord, thank You for Your attention to those who struggle. I do not pretend to understand Your ways. They are higher and greater than my own. Help me never to question why You act in one way here and another there. When I question Your provision, I question Your sovereignty. You work in ways I cannot know. Help me to trust that You remain Jehovah-Jireh, the One who provides, regardless of the timing or the methods You may choose. Amen.

The Best Approach

Father, help me to be given a special ability that knows the best approach. I have seen parents scream at their children. I don't think that works. I have seen husbands and wives who keep everything separate and basically live just as roommates. I don't want that for my marriage. God, when dealing with conflict in my workplace, I so often speak without consulting You. Help me to seek You daily that I might approach issues such as these in the best manner possible. Thank You, Father. Amen.

Day 157

Good Things

God, You are the Giver of all good things. You withhold no precious gift from Your children. Wonderful gifts flow down from You even though we are not deserving. Just as an earthly father longs to give to his children and provide for them, You long to bless us. All that we have comes from You. Make us good stewards of good things, I pray. Amen.

When we were overwhelmed by sins,
you forgave our transgressions.
Blessed are those you choose
and bring near to live in your courts!
We are filled with the good things of
your house, of your holy temple.

PSALM 65:3–4 NIV

Day 158

To Be Humble

Father, You've given me the wonderful task of being a mother. Help me to do the job humbly and to rely on You. That is what would please You most, and that reward is the best motivator I could ask for. Humble me that I might be lifted up. I ask this in the name of Jesus, who died for me. Amen.

Humble yourselves before the Lord, and he will lift you up.

JAMES 4:10 NIV

Day 159

Surrounded by Love

Lord, Your promise of protection gives me a secure feeling. I'm surrounded by Your love and protection. Because You love me and care for me, I can do the same for my children. Thank You for the peace this brings. Amen.

But I am like an olive tree flourishing in the house of God; I trust in God's unfailing love for ever and ever.

PSALM 52:8 NIV

Day 160

The Mighty One

Father, as long as I trust in Your presence, I have nothing to worry about. Nothing can separate me from You, because You are the strong Protector, the mighty One who watches over me always. I praise You, Lord, for Your protection. Amen.

But let all who take refuge in you be glad; let them ever sing for joy. Spread your protection over them, that those who love your name may rejoice in you.

PSALM 5:11 NIV

Day 161

Heart Friends

Lord, You know how painful it is when things are not right between friends. What a joy it is to know that I am made right with You by faith. We can communicate freely, talking and listening, enjoying each other as heart friends. Thank You for restoration and righteousness. In Jesus' name I pray, amen.

Since, then, you have been raised with Christ, set your hearts on things above, where Christ is, seated at the right hand of God.

COLOSSIANS 3:1 NIV

Day 162

Your Promises

- -

Thank You, Lord, that Your Word is true. Help me to look to Your steady and solid Word, not this world, as my life instruction manual. I thank You that You will never lead me astray, that You never lie to me, and that You always keep Your promises. Amen.

Let us hold unswervingly to the hope we profess, for he who promised is faithful.

HEBREWS 10:23 NIV

Day 163

To Be Pure

- -

Lord, on days when I'm having spiritual struggles, my thoughts become full of discouragement and frustration. I don't like to be so controlled by my emotions. Please give me the strength to be pure in every situation. Amen.

Finally, brothers and sisters, whatever
is true, whatever is noble, whatever
is right, whatever is pure, whatever is
lovely, whatever is admirable—
if anything is excellent or praiseworthy—
think about such things.

PHILIPPIANS 4:8 NIV

Day 164

Reflections

Lord, help me realize that everything my husband says about me does not always reflect his true feelings. When his words hurt me, show me how to explain this to him. I am "a good thing"—I deserve to be treated with respect. Amen.

Husbands, in the same way be considerate as you live with your wives, and treat them with respect as the weaker partner and as heirs with you of the gracious gift of life, so that nothing will hinder your prayers.

1 PETER 3:7 NIV

Day 165

Control My Tongue, Lord

- -

Lord, in the heat of anger, control my tongue,
because what I say then can be as damaging
to my soul as it is to my victim's reputation.
Remove from me the temptation to gossip, for
no good comes from this. Make me faithful in
all things, Lord. Amen.

Women must likewise be dignified,
not malicious gossips, but temperate,
faithful in all things.

1 TIMOTHY 3:11 NASB

Day 166

Made Worthy

Lord, You stand before the throne of Your
Father and claim me as Your own, exempt
from sin and judgment. Because of Your sacrifice, I am made worthy. Because You were
presented as the spotless Lamb of God, I am
seen as righteous by my Father. He sees me
through a "Jesus lens." Thank You. Amen.

When you have finished cleansing it, you
shall present a young bull without blemish
and a ram without blemish from the flock.

EZEKIEL 43:23 NASB

Day 167

Blameless

God, sometimes I slip up or make a mistake. I sin without meaning to do so. Other times, I am tempted and I follow Satan's detour willingly. I move away from You and I seek things that are unhealthy and not godly. This can bring great destruction to my life. I have seen it in others' lives as they have crumbled away. I don't want this for my life. Make me blameless before You. Keep me from willful sin, I pray. Amen.

Keep your servant also from willful sins; may they not rule over me. Then I will be blameless, innocent of great transgression.

PSALM 19:13 NIV

Day 168

My Prayer Life

Lord, I long to be more connected to You. Teach me to worship You as the true Source of power and love. I adore You like no other. Transform me so my prayers will be powerful and my life will be fruitful. Amen.

Therefore, confess your sins to one another, and pray for one another so that you may be healed. The effective prayer of a righteous man can accomplish much.

JAMES 5:16 NASB

Day 169

What a Blessing!

Thank You, Lord, for putting other godly women in my life. They face many temptations and struggles that I face, but they've committed themselves to purity and godliness, so together we can encourage one another. What a blessing it is to have a circle of Christian friends! Help me never to take them for granted and remind me to lift them up in prayer regularly. Amen.

A friend loves at all times,
And a brother is born for adversity.

PROVERBS 17:17 NASB

Source of Hope

- -

Lord, so many times I am tempted to think that people or things will satisfy me. But often they leave me empty and unfulfilled. Help me to remember that You are the Source of my hope—not a man, or a better job, or a pan of brownies! You are my God, my Creator. You are not far away, but You are living right here in my heart. All I need to do is turn to You and call on You in times of need. Amen.

Day 171

Patient Endurance

Thank You, Lord. You have given me a wonderful example of patient endurance. When I am losing patience with my children, I recall how long You waited for me to repent and turn to You. Amen.

The Lord is not slow about His promise, as some count slowness, but is patient toward you, not wishing for any to perish but for all to come to repentance.

2 PETER 3:9 NASB

Day 172

A New Creation in Christ

Lord, now that I am devoted to You heart and
soul, I am a new creation. Thank You for washing
away my old ways of thinking and behaving,
and for empowering me to live a new life. Your
love changes me! Amen.

Therefore, if anyone is in Christ,
the new creation has come: The old
has gone, the new is here!

2 CORINTHIANS 5:17 NIV

Day 173

Help Me to Wait

Father, when my children do wrong, I want them to admit it and ask for forgiveness. From Your example with me, I know there are times when I need to wait for my children's repentance. Help me to wait, Lord. Amen.

Whoever is patient has great understanding, but one who is quick-tempered displays folly.
PROVERBS 14:29 NIV

Heal Me, Lord

Thank You for the times when I am humbled, Lord. You are always here—to listen, to forgive, and to heal. Lord, help me to be repentant, to be willing to be brought low. Heal me, Lord. Heal me of quick-temperedness and selfishness. They are as powerful as deadly diseases that threaten our physical lives. They have the power to bring destruction to my heart and soul. Heal this waywardness in me, I pray. Amen.

Day 175

The Right Example

Lord, when I am old, I want my children to respect and love me. By my actions toward others, I am always teaching—either respect or disrespect. I want to set the right example for my children as I honor older people. Amen.

"Stand up in the presence of the aged,
show respect for the elderly and
revere your God. I am the LORD."

LEVITICUS 19:32 NIV

Day 176

Humble Me

- -

Humble me, Lord. Fill me with the desire to hearken to my parents. I can learn so much from them and benefit from their life experiences. I believe this is Your will. Thank You for Your patience and guidance. Amen.

"Honor your father and your mother,
as the LORD your God has commanded you,
so that you may live long and that it may
go well with you in the land the LORD
your God is giving you."

DEUTERONOMY 5:16 NIV

Day 177

On Level Ground

- -

God, the society in which I live is shaky. It is unsteady and unstable. The fashions and priorities shift with the days. I want to build my house upon the stability of Your Word. I want to do Your will even in a world that says it is fine to do as I feel. Please lead me on level ground. Make my way straight before me and teach me to look neither left or right, but to follow hard after my God. Amen.

Teach me to do your will, for you are my God; may your good Spirit lead me on level ground.

PSALM 143:10 NIV

Day 178

Great Expectations

Lord, You've given me a life that abounds with rich blessings, and You've guaranteed that because of this You also have great expectations of me. Help me to be faithful to these expectations. Amen.

"But the one who does not know and does things deserving punishment will be beaten with few blows. From everyone who has been given much, much will be demanded; and from the one who has been entrusted with much, much more will be asked."

LUKE 12:48 NIV

The Humble Spirit

- -

Heavenly Father, we live in a world that lifts up proud people. Make us all aware of how much You value sacrifice. Help us to have the humble spirit we need when we come before You. Amen.

He has told you, O man, what is good;
and what does the LORD require of you
but to do justice, to love kindness,
and to walk humbly with your God?

MICAH 6:8 NASB

Day 180

For Your Mercy

Thank You, Jesus, for calling sinners to repentance. If You had come only for the righteous, I would not have been called, for I am a sinner. I thank You for Your mercy. Amen.

Then it happened that as Jesus was reclining at the table in the house, behold, many tax collectors and sinners came and were dining with Jesus and His disciples.

MATTHEW 9:10 NASB

A Prayer from Priscilla Shirer's Heart

But I say his reign of terror stops here. Stops now. He might keep coming, but he won't have victory anymore. Because it all starts failing when we start praying.

—from *Fervent: A Woman's Battle Plan for Serious, Specific, and Strategic Prayer*

Day 182

Growing Spiritually

Lord, I want to grow up spiritually. I want to move from head knowledge to heart experience with You. I want to know what it means to enjoy Your presence, not just to make requests. Step by step and day by day, teach me to follow and learn Your ways. Amen.

When I was a child, I used to speak like a child, think like a child, reason like a child; when I became a man, I did away with childish things.

1 CORINTHIANS 13:11 NASB

Day 183

Taking Up My Cross

Lord, here I am before You. I am ready to "take up my cross" and follow You. Every day I want to be with You, empowered by You, and loved so deeply that I am changed. Show me what it means to lose my life in order to save it. Amen.

And He was saying to them all,
"If anyone wishes to come after Me,
he must deny himself, and take up
his cross daily and follow Me."

LUKE 9:23 NASB

Day 184

Godly Responses

Lord, what a blessing You are that You have given us such an array of emotions with which to express ourselves. Help me to be more like You—slow to anger and abounding in love. Help me to be a woman who is forgiving. Amen.

*"But You are a God of forgiveness,
gracious and compassionate,
slow to anger and abounding
in lovingkindness;
and You did not forsake them."*

NEHEMIAH 9:17 NASB

Day 185

Everywhere

Lord, there is so much I do not understand about You. Still, I can see the effects of Your actions, the evidence that You are still active in my daily life. I do not need to physically see You to believe. Your evidence is everywhere. Amen.

For since the creation of the world His invisible attributes, His eternal power and divine nature, have been clearly seen, being understood through what has been made, so that they are without excuse.

ROMANS 1:20 NASB

Day 186

Whole

Father, the life I am living right now is not the result of my faith in You but of Your faith in me. Thank You for Your sacrifice, which saves me and makes me whole. Amen.

Consider it all joy, my brethren,
when you encounter various trials,
knowing that the testing of your faith
produces endurance. And let endurance
have its perfect result, so that you may be
perfect and complete, lacking in nothing.

JAMES 1:2–4 NASB

Day 187

Heart of Compassion

- -

Lord, Your compassion for people is great. Create in me a heart of compassion—enlarge my vision so I see and help the poor, the sick, the people who don't know You, and the people whose concerns You lay upon my heart. Just as You are gracious and compassionate, teach me to overflow with grace and mercy to those around me, I pray. Amen.

The LORD is gracious and righteous;
our God is full of compassion.
PSALM 116:5 NIV

Example of Compassion

Lord, help me to show compassion for my children and also for strangers. You were the best example. You loved everyone, Lord. You gave Your life for all people. Help me do the same, and in doing so set an example for my children. Amen.

But the angel said to them, "Do not be afraid. I bring you good news that will cause great joy for all the people."

LUKE 2:10 NIV

Day 189

No More Hiding

- -

Lord, I can no longer hide in the darkness of
my guilt and sin. You already know everything
I've done wrong, yet You bring me into the
light—not to condemn, nor to condone, but
to heal me. I acknowledge my wrongs and
confess them all to You, Lord. Amen.

Woe to those who go to great depths
to hide their plans from the LORD,
who do their work in darkness and think,
"Who sees us? Who will know?"

ISAIAH 29:15 NIV

Day 190

Victory over Death

Lord, thank You for Your gift of eternal life
and the power to do Your will. I cannot fathom
how You suffered, yet You did it all for me—for
every person. You bled for my sins. You had
victory over death. You made a way for me.
Thank You, Lord. Amen.

*The sting of death is sin, and the power of
sin is the law. But thanks be to God! He gives
us the victory through our Lord Jesus Christ.*

1 CORINTHIANS 15:56–57 NIV

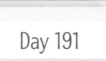

Day 191

A Light to My Path

- -

Lord, Your Word is a lamp in my darkness—a flashlight on the path of life that helps me see the way. Your words enlighten me with wisdom, insight, and hope, even when I cannot see where I am going or how things will turn out. Thank You. Amen.

Your word is a lamp to my feet
and a light to my path.

PSALM 119:105 NASB

Day 192

Heaven and Earth

God, Your thoughts are as far above mine as the heavens are above the earth. It is hard for me to fathom that You spoke all of this into existence—the trees and flowers of all kinds, animals in all their uniqueness, even human beings. You have given man so much authority and responsibility in Your world. Help us to be wise stewards of Your creation. Amen.

"LORD, the God of Israel, enthroned between the cherubim, you alone are God over all the kingdoms of the earth. You have made heaven and earth."

2 KINGS 19:15 NIV

Day 193

A Joyful Noise

- -

Lord, You are my strength and my song. Help me teach my children to sing, no matter what is going on around us. I want us to make a joyful noise to You, Jesus, the Author and Finisher of our faith. Amen.

Shout joyfully to the LORD, all the earth. Serve the LORD with gladness; come before Him with joyful singing. Know that the LORD Himself is God; it is He who has made us, and not we ourselves; we are His people and the sheep of His pasture.

PSALM 100:1–3 NASB

Health

Lord, thank You for my good health. I pray for Your power to sustain me as I take care of myself—by eating healthy food, drinking enough water, and making movement and exercise a part of my daily life. Please keep me from injury and illness. When I do suffer illness, Father, I pray that You will use that time to draw me closer to You. Sometimes, as a busy woman, I must be halted by illness in order to find time to rest and seek You. Help me to take the necessary time that my body needs to heal. Amen.

Day 195

Self-Control

God, self-control is not one of my strengths, and I need to work on it. Help me turn things over to You and allow You to develop self-control in my life. Amen.

Now for this very reason also, applying all diligence, in your faith supply moral excellence, and in your moral excellence, knowledge, and in your knowledge, self-control, and in your self-control, perseverance, and in your perseverance, godliness, and in your godliness, brotherly kindness, and in your brotherly kindness, love. For if these qualities are yours and are increasing, they render you neither useless nor unfruitful in the true knowledge of our Lord Jesus Christ.

2 PETER 1:5–8 NASB

Day 196

Quiet My Spirit

- -

Lord, there's so much chaos. Quiet my spirit. Let me close my eyes for a moment and experience Your touch. My strength comes from You, not from any other source. Calm me. Keep me anchored in You and Your Spirit. Amen.

"The steadfast of mind You will keep in perfect peace, because he trusts in You."

ISAIAH 26:3 NASB

Day 197

Know My Heart

God, no one else can see my heart. They may get glimpses of it through my words or actions. They may grow to know me well over the years. But You are my Creator. You knit me together in the secret place within my mother's womb. You know my heart. Make it pure, Father. I long to have a pure heart before You. Amen.

Search me, God, and know my heart;
test me and know my anxious thoughts.
See if there is any offensive way in me,
and lead me in the way everlasting.

PSALM 139:23–24 NIV

Day 198

Help with Parenting

Lord, when I first considered starting a family,
I thought I would be a perfect parent. It was
easier dreamed than done. I know I need Your
assistance if I'm going to be a good mother. I'm
so grateful for Your guidance. Amen.

Behold, children are a gift of the LORD,
the fruit of the womb is a reward.

PSALM 127:3 NASB

God's Strength

Because of Your strength, Lord, I can smile.
When I need peace, You strengthen me on the
inside. This is where I need You the most. Let
me reflect Your strength so that my children
and those around me will be drawn to You also.
I am not strong on my own, but in You, O Lord,
I am more than a conqueror. Amen.

Day 200

Mentors

Lord, thank You for the older women in my life who have been mentors to me. Teach me to love my husband and children, to be self-controlled and pure, to be kind, and to know Your Word—so that I can teach what is good to other women around me. May we continue to encourage one another in the faith. Amen.

Therefore encourage one another and build up one another, just as you also are doing.

1 THESSALONIANS 5:11 NASB

Day 201

Blessed Promise

Father, physically, I'm wearing out. But in the core of my being, in my heart, I still feel strengthened by You. What a blessed promise, that this inner strength will be my portion forever. Amen.

For we know that when this earthly tent we live in is taken down (that is, when we die and leave this earthly body), we will have a house in heaven, an eternal body made for us by God himself and not by human hands.

2 CORINTHIANS 5:1 NLT

Day 202

Awesome God

God, the word *awesome* has become so over-used in the society in which I live. We call everything from sports teams to musical artists "awesome." We say that a certain type of pizza or a kindness shown by a friend is "awesome." Help us to be cautious as to what truly leaves us in awe. You, God, the Creator of all and Redeemer of my heart. . .You are truly awesome! Amen.

You, God, are awesome in your sanctuary; the God of Israel gives power and strength to his people. Praise be to God!

PSALM 68:35 NIV

Day 203

Angels Watching over Me

Lord, I thank You that You are my true companion—that I am never alone. You have assigned angels to watch over and protect me. You have given me Your Holy Spirit and promised that You are with me always, even to the very end of the age. Amen.

For He will give His angels
charge concerning you,
to guard you in all your ways.

PSALM 91:11 NASB

Cornerstone

Lord, I ask that You would establish our home on the solid rock of Your love. Be our cornerstone. May our family be rooted in love, grounded in grace, and rich in respect for one another. May we stand firm as a family built on a foundation of true faith. In Jesus' name I pray, amen.

*Therefore thus says the Lord GOD,
"Behold, I am laying in Zion a stone,
a tested stone, a costly cornerstone
for the foundation, firmly placed. He
who believes in it will not be disturbed."*

ISAIAH 28:16 NASB

That Wonderful Day

- -

Lord, I know there will come a day when we will be in heaven with You. I look forward to that time, and I thank You for the opportunity to share that time and place with You. Just as the criminal who died on the cross next to Yours, I will be with You in Paradise because I believe in You. What a promise! Amen.

And He said to him, "Truly I say to you, today you shall be with Me in Paradise."

LUKE 23:43 NASB

Day 206

Creative Delight

Father, I want to make You exciting and inter-esting to my children. Give me creative ideas as we take walks, clean the house, do schoolwork, or engage in other routine activities. I pray it will be a delight for all of us. Amen.

I was very glad to find some of your children walking in truth, just as we have received commandment to do from the Father.

2 JOHN 1:4 NASB

A Hedge of Protection

Lord, be our strong defense and protect our home. May this be a place of safety, comfort, and peace. Guard us from outside forces and protect us from harmful attacks from within. I pray that the Holy Spirit would put a hedge of protection around our home and family. In Jesus' name I pray, amen.

"You have always put a wall of protection around him and his home and his property. You have made him prosper in everything he does."

JOB 1:10 NLT

Day 208

Joy of Celebration

Lord, thank You for the joy of celebration! Help us to be a family that remembers and gathers together—not just for birthdays and holidays, but even to celebrate the little blessings of life. We are thankful for all that You have done in our lives. Amen.

So let us celebrate the festival, not with the old bread of wickedness and evil, but with the new bread of sincerity and truth.

1 CORINTHIANS 5:8 NLT

Day 209

Eyes on Jesus

In the midst of suffering, I want to keep my eyes on You, Jesus. The suffering You endured for my sake makes my trials looks like nothing. Help me look forward to the promise and forget the temporary troubles I have now. *When I turn my eyes upon Jesus and look full in Your wonderful face, the things of earth grow strangely dim in the light of Your glory and grace!* Amen.

Day 210

Joy Even in Trials

Lord, it seems odd to consider trials a joyful thing. But I pray that my challenges in life, these times of testing, will lead me to greater perseverance. May that perseverance finish its work so I will be mature and complete, on my way to wholeness. Amen.

"I have told you all this so that you may have peace in me. Here on earth you will have many trials and sorrows. But take heart, because I have overcome the world."

JOHN 16:33 NLT

A Prayer from Susanna Wesley's Heart

You, O Lord, have called us to watch and pray. Therefore, whatever may be the sin against which we pray, make us careful to watch against it, and so have reason to expect that our prayers will be answered. In order to perform this duty aright, grant us grace to preserve a sober, equal temper, and sincerity to pray for Your assistance. Amen.

Day 212

The Good Times

Lord, I ask for Your help when it comes to getting along with my family members. Teach me to focus on the good times we had together, not the bad, and to concentrate on their good points for the sake of family peace. Thank You for adopting us into Your family. Amen.

God decided in advance to adopt us into his own family by bringing us to himself through Jesus Christ. This is what he wanted to do, and it gave him great pleasure.

EPHESIANS 1:5 NLT

Day 213

Unfailing Love

Lord, we humans fail one another. I fail my husband and children. I fail my employer. It just comes with the territory of living in a fallen world. I thank You for Your unfailing love. It is unconditional, and it is the same yesterday, today, and tomorrow. I rejoice as Your child that I can always count on You. Amen.

But I trust in your unfailing love;
my heart rejoices in your salvation.
PSALM 13:5 NIV

Day 214

Your Word Is Like Rain

Lord, thank You for Your words that speak to my heart and needs. Your life-giving messages are like rain showers on new, green grass. I need not just a sprinkle, but a downpour—a soaking, abundant rain in my dry heart! Amen.

"Let my teaching fall on you like rain;
let my speech settle like dew.
Let my words fall like rain on tender grass,
like gentle showers on young plants."

DEUTERONOMY 32:2 NLT

Eternal Blessings of Discipline

Father, Your correction lasts only a moment; but its blessings are eternal. When I realize You are so concerned for me and want to help me, I am filled with gratitude and willing to be led in the right direction. You discipline me as I discipline my children, out of love. Amen.

"Think about it: Just as a parent disciplines a child, the LORD your God disciplines you for your own good."

DEUTERONOMY 8:5 NLT

Day 216

Sharing the Gift

God, my responsibility as Your child is to share the gift of salvation with others. So many need to hear the Gospel. Make me attentive to each opportunity You present to me. Amen.

Then Jesus came to them and said, "All authority in heaven and on earth has been given to me. Therefore go and make disciples of all nations, baptizing them in the name of the Father and of the Son and of the Holy Spirit, and teaching them to obey everything I have commanded you. And surely I am with you always, to the very end of the age."

MATTHEW 28:18–20 NIV

Day 217

Secure in Love

Father, I pray I will be able to bear death as well as I bore life, secure in Your love and looking to the salvation that You have promised is mine. Amen.

"Do not let your hearts be troubled. You believe in God; believe also in me. My Father's house has many rooms; if that were not so, would I have told you that I am going there to prepare a place for you? And if I go and prepare a place for you, I will come back and take you to be with me that you also may be where I am."

JOHN 14:1–3 NIV

Day 218

One True God

You are the one true God. You are the Great I Am, faithful in every situation to be what we need You to be. You provide. You sustain. You forgive. You teach and guide and even discipline Your children in love. You are the Good Shepherd. There is no one like You. I praise Your name today and forevermore! Amen.

"LORD, the God of Israel, there is no God like you in heaven above or on earth below—you who keep your covenant of love with your servants who continue wholeheartedly in your way."

1 KINGS 8:23 NIV

Dreams and Desires

Dear Giver of dreams, I believe You've placed dreams within me that are yet to be realized. Teach me to delight myself in You as I pursue the desires of my heart. Show me Your perfect will—may I move as far and as fast as You wish. May Your perfect will be carried out in my life as I submit all things to You. Amen.

Take delight in the LORD, and he will give you your heart's desires.

PSALM 37:4 NLT

Day 220

Confidence

Father, cleanse me from my ungrounded fears. Fill me with confidence that I can share with my children. You are the strong Protector. I am thankful that, because of Jesus, we will be lifted up as the stones in a crown. Amen.

On that day the LORD their God will rescue his people, just as a shepherd rescues his sheep. They will sparkle in his land like jewels in a crown.

ZECHARIAH 9:16 NLT

Standing Firm

Lord, show my children what convictions to establish and give them the strength to stand firm in those convictions. Even if an activity or custom is permissible, it may not be of benefit. Help my children to be discerning as they make decisions regarding their lifestyles. I ask this in Jesus' name, amen.

But he who doubts is condemned if he eats, because his eating is not from faith; and whatever is not from faith is sin.

ROMANS 14:23 NASB

A Light to Others

Lord, may those I work with always see You in my life and be brought closer to You through me. I never want to be a stumbling block but always a beacon of light that leads others to You. If they ask me about the joy in my life, please give me the courage to boldly speak the name of Jesus and to share the Gospel with them. Give me opportunities for spiritual conversations, I pray. Amen.

Day 223

Praise the Lord!

- -

Lord, may all creation praise You as I praise You. Amen.

Let every created thing give praise to the LORD, for he issued his command, and they came into being. He set them in place forever and ever. His decree will never be revoked. Praise the LORD from the earth, you creatures of the ocean depths, fire and hail, snow and clouds, wind and weather that obey him, mountains and all hills, fruit trees and all cedars, wild animals and all livestock, small scurrying animals and birds.

PSALM 148:5–10 NLT

Day 224

The Promise

Thank You for Your promise to guide me in all things great and small. Your eye is always on me, keeping me from error and ensuring that I can always find a way home to You. Amen.

The LORD is watching everywhere, keeping his eye on both the evil and the good.

PROVERBS 15:3 NLT

But the eyes of the LORD are on those who fear him, on those whose hope is in his unfailing love.

PSALM 33:18 NIV

Day 225

God's Perfect Will

Lord, I commit my aspirations to You. Give me the courage to work toward my own goals and not be swayed by the opinions of others. Renew my mind and spirit so I will be able to test and approve what Your will is—Your good, pleasing, and perfect will. Amen.

Do not conform to the pattern of this world, but be transformed by the renewing of your mind. Then you will be able to test and approve what God's will is—his good, pleasing and perfect will.

ROMANS 12:2 NIV

Day 226

You Know the Way, Lord

Lord, I do not know how to deliver myself from temptation, but You know the way. You have been there. When I stumble, I know Your arms will catch me; if I fall, You bring me to my feet and guide me onward. Amen.

*For though the righteous fall
seven times, they rise again, but the
wicked stumble when calamity strikes.*

PROVERBS 24:16 NIV

Saved by Grace

- -

Lord, You give the best gifts! I receive the love gift of my salvation, knowing that it is by grace that I have been saved, through faith. I didn't do anything to deserve it or earn it. Instead, You saved me by grace so I can now do good works. Amen.

For it is by grace you have been saved, through faith—and this is not from yourselves, it is the gift of God—not by works, so that no one can boast.

EPHESIANS 2:8–9 NIV

Day 228

Great Peace

Lord, You have given me a peace that allows me to live confidently in this world. Even if people disagree with my beliefs, even if I am persecuted or belittled, I will rest in Your peace. Nothing has the power to come against me, because I am Your child. I love Your law and I seek to follow it. In Jesus' name, amen.

Great peace have those who love your law, and nothing can make them stumble.

PSALM 119:165 NIV

Day 229

Peace, Forgiveness, and Love

Lord, forgive me when I treat my family members poorly. Show me their good points, for I have overlooked or forgotten many of them. For the sake of our parents, our children, and ourselves, help me bring peace, forgiveness, and love to our family. Amen.

Be completely humble and gentle; be patient, bearing with one another in love.

EPHESIANS 4:2 NIV

Day 230

Simple Service

Father, there comes a time in every woman's life when her parents begin to need help. Give me the wisdom to understand the problems they are having and the often-simple ways I can be of service to them. Amen.

"Honor your father and mother"—which is the first commandment with a promise— "so that it may go well with you and that you may enjoy long life on the earth."

EPHESIANS 6:2–3 NIV

Day 231

Constantly Blessed

Lord, I know bad things will come my way in life, but I am secure in Your love, which never fails. I am constantly blessed by Your care and concern. I am so important to You that even the hairs of my head are all numbered. Remind me that I am not immune to the troubles of this world. I am thankful that You have already overcome this world! Amen.

Beyond Beauty

Lord, teach me to look through appearance when I choose my friends or my husband. Help me see beyond beauty—or lack of it. It is what is on the inside that counts. Amen.

Rather, it should be that of your inner self, the unfading beauty of a gentle and quiet spirit, which is of great worth in God's sight.

1 PETER 3:4 NIV

Do not be misled: "Bad company corrupts good character."

1 CORINTHIANS 15:33 NIV

Day 233

God Is Worthy

You created all things, and in You, all things
have their being. You are the Creator of the
universe. You are worthy of praise and honor.
May I never take You for granted or speak to
You casually. Yes, You are my Abba Father,
but You are also the Sovereign God of the
world. You are my King, worthy of more glory
and honor than I am capable of giving. Amen.

*"You are worthy, our Lord and God,
to receive glory and honor and power,
for you created all things, and by your will
they were created and have their being."*

REVELATION 4:11 NIV

Day 234

Money Matters

Father, when it comes to money matters, I cannot approach perfection, but I know that with Your help I can learn to handle our family finances faithfully. Guide me in Your wisdom and set before me wise counselors as needed. Amen.

"The man who had received five bags of gold went at once and put his money to work and gained five bags more."

MATTHEW 25:16 NIV

Day 235

Father, Direct Me

Father, direct me in how to be involved in the lives of my children. Help me build on Your teachings by setting the right example, praying for them, being there for them, and caring for them. Amen.

"Fix these words of mine in your hearts and minds; tie them as symbols on your hands and bind them on your foreheads. Teach them to your children, talking about them when you sit at home and when you walk along the road, when you lie down and when you get up."

DEUTERONOMY 11:18–19 NIV

Day 236

The Call of Motherhood

Lord, I believe the call to motherhood comes from You. Help me approach my calling with a meek and humble spirit. Only when my outlook becomes Christlike will I truly be considered worthy of this calling. Amen.

"Their descendants will be known among the nations and their offspring among the peoples. All who see them will acknowledge that they are a people the LORD has blessed."

ISAIAH 61:9 NIV

Day 237

Bread of Heaven

Lord, I need Your times of refreshing in my life.
Bread of Heaven, as You nourish my body with
food, feed my soul with Your words of comfort
and life. May I be filled with Your healing love,
joy, and goodness. Amen.

*"I am the living bread that came down
from heaven. Whoever eats this bread will
live forever. This bread is my flesh, which I
will give for the life of the world."*

JOHN 6:51 NIV

Hospitality

- -

Lord, thank You for my home. Show me opportunities to open this home to others. However my home compares with others', I thank You for what I have. I am grateful that Your Spirit is present here. Give me a generous, open heart, and use my home for Your purposes. Amen.

*Do not neglect to show hospitality
to strangers, for by this some have
entertained angels without knowing it.*

HEBREWS 13:2 NASB

Transform My Mind

Lord, sometimes I feel like my emotions need a makeover. Renovate me—transform me so I can be balanced and healthy emotionally. I ask for Your power to change. I don't want to be the way I used to be. I want to be wise and enjoy sound thinking. Amen.

And we all, who with unveiled faces contemplate the Lord's glory, are being transformed into his image with ever-increasing glory, which comes from the Lord, who is the Spirit.

2 CORINTHIANS 3:18 NIV

Honor

Father, sometimes I have to go against the wishes of others to do Your will, and it's not always pleasant, but Your wishes come before all others, and I will do my best to honor Your name all my days. You are worthy of honor. Amen.

*"Amen!
Praise and glory and wisdom
and thanks and honor and
power and strength be to our
God for ever and ever. Amen!"*
REVELATION 7:12 NIV

A Prayer from Amy Carmichael's Heart

And shall I pray Thee change Thy will, my Father, Until it be according unto mine? But no, Lord, no, that shall never be, rather I pray Thee blend my human will with Thine. I pray Thee hush the hurrying eager longing I pray Thee soothe the pangs of keen desire. See in my quiet places wishes thronging, Forbid them, Lord, purge, though it be with fire. And work in me to will and do Thy pleasure. Let all within me, peaceful, reconciled, Tarry content my Wellbeloved's leisure, At last, at last, even as a weaned child.

Day 242

Never on My Own

Lord, I know that You are the One at work in me; Your Spirit is a part of me, and You guide my thoughts and actions. Thank You for that. I don't know what I would do if I had to live life on my own. Amen.

"I will lead the blind by ways they have not known, along unfamiliar paths I will guide them; I will turn the darkness into light before them and make the rough places smooth. These are the things I will do; I will not forsake them."

ISAIAH 42:16 NIV

My Body

Lord, help me to be a person who takes care of herself. Help me to make wise decisions and to be a good steward of myself, the "temple" You have given me. Help me not to abuse my body, but to care for it as You would want me to. Amen.

Do you not know that your bodies are temples of the Holy Spirit, who is in you, whom you have received from God? You are not your own; you were bought at a price. Therefore honor God with your bodies.

1 CORINTHIANS 6:19–20 NIV

Day 244

Marriage

Lord, I ask that my husband and I would value each other. As he loves me, help me to respect him. As I value him, help him to cherish me. Teach us to give and to receive in the ways that are meaningful to each of us. Amen.

Now as the church submits to Christ, so also wives should submit to their husbands in everything. Husbands, love your wives, just as Christ loved the church and gave himself up for her to make her holy, cleansing her by the washing with water through the word.

EPHESIANS 5:24–26 NIV

Day 245

Cast Your Cares

Lord, I do not just hand You my concerns. I will do as You instruct me. I will cast my worries at the foot of Your throne. I will toss them there deliberately, trusting You to handle them. I refuse to pick them back up this time. Create in me a trust that is like none I have ever experienced. Help me to trust You instead of worrying. Amen.

Cast your cares on the Lord
and he will sustain you; he will
never let the righteous be shaken.
PSALM 55:22 NIV

Day 246

Fill Me with Comfort

Father, my heart is breaking over the death of someone I love. Fill me with Your comfort and the joy that comes from knowing that when death does come, You will be there to guide us home to You. I claim the comfort that You promise in Your Word. Amen.

"Blessed are those who mourn,
for they will be comforted."

MATTHEW 5:4 NIV

A Lighter Heart

- -

Lord, buoy my spirits. I need more joy in my life. Daily living and trials can be so depleting; I just can't do it on my own. Help me to laugh more and enjoy life again. Help me to have a childlike, playful spirit—a lighter heart, Lord. Amen.

"You have made known to me the paths of life; you will fill me with joy in your presence."

ACTS 2:28 NIV

Nothing Is Impossible

Father, quite often I pray for what is impossible. But for You, nothing is impossible. Even where there seems to be no way, You can make a way. Help me to trust in You to do the impossible in my life. Then, when blessings come, remind me to give You all the honor and glory. In Jesus' name I pray, amen.

"For nothing will be impossible with God."

LUKE 1:37 NASB

Day 249

Restoration

Lord, thank You for the peace that restores me and brings wholeness. When my heart is restless, my health suffers. But when I am at peace, You restore my entire body. I can breathe easier, and I can smile again because I know everything's going to be all right. Amen.

Then they cried out to the LORD in their trouble; He saved them out of their distresses. He sent His word and healed them, and delivered them from their destructions.

PSALM 107:19–20 NASB

Something Special

Heavenly Father, I pray that my children will love Your Word and understand how special they are to You and that You have something for each of them to meditate on each day. Draw them close to You, Father. Help us to glorify You as a family. As we set apart time for devotions together, may we grow spiritually side by side. Each member of our family is special to You, and You have great plans for us. Amen.

Day 251

Obedient Heart

Lord, Your Word says that if we obey Your commands, we will remain in Your love. I want to serve You out of an obedient, not a rebellious, heart. Just as Jesus submits to You, Father, I choose to submit to You too. Obedience leads to a blessing. Amen.

And He said to them, "Where is your faith?" They were fearful and amazed, saying to one another, "Who then is this, that He commands even the winds and the water, and they obey Him?"

LUKE 8:25 NASB

Day 252

Supportive

Father, help me remember that my priorities are not necessarily the priorities of those I love, so please give me the sense to step back and allow everyone a little leeway to lead their own lives. Give me eyes to see the unique gifts and personalities of each member of my family. Help me to appreciate their dreams and goals even if they are not my own. Help me be supportive, not bossy. Amen.

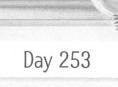

Rest

- -

Lord, I need rest. I am so tired and worn out.
Help me sleep well at night. I ask for more
energy during the day and a more vibrant
spirit. Lighten my load so I can have a better
balance between my work, ministry, and home
life. Replenish me, Lord. Amen.

*By the seventh day God completed
His work which He had done, and He
rested on the seventh day from all
His work which He had done.*

GENESIS 2:2 NASB

Day 254

The Future

Lord, thank You for giving me hope. I don't know what the future holds, but You give me the ability to be joyful even while I wait. Please help me to live with a mind-set of patience and courage as You work Your will in my life. Amen.

"For I know the plans I have for you,"
declares the LORD, "plans to prosper
you and not to harm you, plans to
give you hope and a future."

JEREMIAH 29:11 NIV

Day 255

Our Nation's Leaders

Lord, we are a hurt nation—an angry nation struggling to maintain its values while still dealing firmly with those who hate us. Guide our nation's leaders during these difficult times. We trust in You and long for peace. Amen.

"You will hear of wars and rumors of wars, but see to it that you are not alarmed. Such things must happen, but the end is still to come."

MATTHEW 24:6 NIV

Day 256

Never Hesitate to Forgive Others

Lord, may I never hesitate to forgive anyone when You have already forgiven me. I am so blessed to be forgiven and made right with God. Amen.

"Therefore, my friends, I want you to know that through Jesus the forgiveness of sins is proclaimed to you. Through him everyone who believes is set free from every sin, a justification you were not able to obtain under the law of Moses."

ACTS 13:38–39 NIV

Day 257

God's Timetable

Father, help me to have patience, knowing my season is coming according to Your timetable and trusting that with Your help, every fruit I produce will be good. Amen.

"For my thoughts are not your thoughts, neither are your ways my ways," declares the LORD. "As the heavens are higher than the earth, so are my ways higher than your ways and my thoughts than your thoughts."

ISAIAH 55:8–9 NIV

Day 258

My Portion

- -

Your Word is my daily nourishment, Lord.
Thank You for the Bread of Life You provide
every single day. Those words feed and nurture my soul. Without Your words I will fade
and die spiritually; with them I am vibrant,
energized, and alive! Be my portion as I seek
You. Amen.

*LORD, you alone are my portion
and my cup; you make my lot secure.*

PSALM 16:5 NIV

Day 259

Remembering God's Ways

Lord Jesus, I thank You for all the times when You have rescued me. I pray that I will always remember Your ways and walk in them. I desperately need Your help to survive and thrive in this dark world. You are my Helper and my gracious, loving, sovereign God. Amen.

You come to the help of
those who gladly do right,
who remember your ways.

ISAIAH 64:5 NIV

Day 260

God's Roles

Lord, You are called Wonderful Counselor because You freely give wisdom and guidance. You are the Mighty God, the One who made the entire world and keeps it all going. My Everlasting Father, it's Your love and compassion that sustain me. My Prince of Peace, I worship and honor You. Amen.

For to us a child is born, to us a son is given, and the government will be on his shoulders. And he will be called Wonderful Counselor, Mighty God, Everlasting Father, Prince of Peace.

Isaiah 9:6 niv

Day 261

Encouragers

- -

Lord, help me to teach my children that to grow as encouragers they can start with small things as they comfort others and build from there. Help me to teach them to use their words appropriately to build others up and not tear them down. Help me to train them to limit sarcasm because it can be hurtful. Most of all, make me a model for these little ones as I seek to encourage them daily. Amen.

Through You, Lord

Through You, Lord, I can live a life that will give others no right to accuse me of any wrong-doing. I pray that You'll allow my life to be an example that will encourage my family, friends, and others to come to You. Amen.

Don't let anyone look down on you because you are young, but set an example for the believers in speech, in conduct, in love, in faith and in purity.

1 TIMOTHY 4:12 NIV

Day 263

The Patience to Wait

Lord, help me to overcome the urge to pat myself on the back in the sight of others. Give me a desire to do good for the sake of doing good and not for praise from those around me. Give me the patience to wait for the day when I will hear You say, "Well done, good and faithful servant." Amen.

Pride goes before destruction,
a haughty spirit before a fall.

PROVERBS 16:18 NIV

Day 264

His Love Endures Forever

----

*Though the LORD is exalted, he looks
kindly on the lowly; though lofty,
he sees them from afar. Though I walk in
the midst of trouble, you preserve my life.
You stretch out your hand against the
anger of my foes; with your right hand
you save me. The LORD will vindicate me;
your love, LORD, endures forever—do not
abandon the works of your hands.*

PSALM 138:6–8 NIV

Firstfruits

Lord, I want our family to pray together more often. We need to put You first because You are the Source of life—and You are worthy of our firstfruits of time and attention. Help us make spending time with You a priority. Amen.

Honor the LORD with your wealth, with the firstfruits of all your crops; then your barns will be filled to overflowing, and your vats will brim over with new wine.

PROVERBS 3:9–10 NIV

Day 266

Overcoming Fears

- -

Lord, being a mother is causing me to worry and be fearful. Thank You for helping me overcome my "mother" fears. I cannot control the future, but I know the One who holds it in His hands. I will trust in You. Life is too wonderful not to enjoy. Amen.

"Therefore do not worry about tomorrow, for tomorrow will worry about itself. Each day has enough trouble of its own."

MATTHEW 6:34 NIV

Day 267

Simple Joys from Above

Lord, thank You for the gift of laughter! Thank You for the joy You bring into my life through a child's smile, a luscious peach, a hot bath, a good night's sleep. Help me remember that when I am "looking up" to You, I can have a more optimistic outlook. Amen.

Every good and perfect gift is from above, coming down from the Father of the heavenly lights, who does not change like shifting shadows.

JAMES 1:17 NIV

Vows

Vows to You must be kept, Father. You not only remember Your promises to us; You never forget our promises to You. Help me treat my vows to You seriously, Lord. If sacrifices are required of me, let me bear them in faith. Amen.

"You will pray to him, and he will hear you, and you will fulfill your vows."

JOB 22:27 NIV

Day 269

An Everlasting Kingdom

----

*The LORD is good to all; he has compassion
on all he has made. All your works praise
you, LORD; your faithful people extol you.
They tell of the glory of your kingdom and
speak of your might, so that all people may
know of your mighty acts and the glorious
splendor of your kingdom. Your kingdom is
an everlasting kingdom, and your dominion
endures through all generations.*

PSALM 145:9–13 NIV

Atmosphere of Love

Lord, help me to give my husband the aid and support he needs. His life is hard, and he deserves to live in an atmosphere of love and security. Amen.

Wives, in the same way submit yourselves to your own husbands so that, if any of them do not believe the word, they may be won over without words by the behavior of their wives.

1 PETER 3:1 NIV

Day 271

A Prayer from Clara H. Scott's Heart

*(Lyrics of her hymn
"Open My Eyes, That I May See")*

Open my eyes, that I may see glimpses of truth Thou hast for me; place in my hands the wonderful key that shall unclasp and set me free. Silently now I wait for Thee, ready, my God, Thy will to see. Open my eyes, illumine me, Spirit divine! Open my mouth, and let me bear gladly the warm truth everywhere; open my heart and let me prepare love with Thy children thus to share. Silently now I wait for Thee, ready, my God, Thy will to see. Open my heart, illumine me, Spirit divine!

Restoring Harmony

Lord, give me the resolve to make things better, to ignore my pride, and to do whatever is needed to restore the harmony in my family. We are a Christian family, and we need to be an example to others and a light in the world. How can we do this if we are not able to get along with one another? I pray for harmony and peace to reign again in my family. Amen.

Day 273

Confidence in His Promises

Lord, give me confidence in Your promises so that I may never worry about the welfare of my children, whom You love even more than I do and have promised to care for. Amen.

Standing on the promises I cannot fall,
Listening every moment to the Spirit's call
Resting in my Savior as my all in all,
Standing on the promises of God.

Day 274

Rescue Me

Lord, rescue me from my sea of doubt and fear. I don't want to be like an ocean wave that is blown and tossed by the wind. Please quiet my stormy emotions and help me believe that You will take care of me. Amen.

Until we all reach unity in the faith and in the knowledge of the Son of God and become mature, attaining to the whole measure of the fullness of Christ. Then we will no longer be infants, tossed back and forth by the waves, and blown here and there by every wind of teaching and by the cunning and craftiness of people in their deceitful scheming.

EPHESIANS 4:13–14 NIV

Good Foods

Lord, thank You for filling the earth with a bounty of food. Help me to make a priority of eating a nutritious blend of foods, to drink enough water, and to avoid overindulging in junk. Help me find food that is healthy and the will to eat in moderation. Amen.

The land produced vegetation: plants bearing seed according to their kinds and trees bearing fruit with seed in it according to their kinds. And God saw that it was good.

GENESIS 1:12 NIV

Day 276

Always Right

Father, I admit that once in a while I have a temper tantrum, disputing Your guidance and wanting my own way, but You have never been wrong. Thank You for Your love and patience, for I will always need Your guidance. Make me more willing to accept the plans You have for me. Deep down, I want what You want for my life and nothing less. Your ways are always right, and You always know what is best. Amen.

Today and Tomorrow

Lord, keep me on the right path when my own plans are flawed, because only You know where You need me to be today and tomorrow. Make my paths straight and steer me clear of any way that would lead me to destruction, I pray. Amen.

There is a way that appears to be right, but in the end it leads to death.

PROVERBS 14:12 NIV

Home

Lord, I often make mistakes on the path of life,
losing sight of the trail and calling out for You.
Thank You for finding me, for putting my feet
back on the path and leading me home. Amen.

*Whoever heeds life-giving correction
will be at home among the wise.*

PROVERBS 15:31 NIV

Day 279

Free Me

God, I often go about my days unaware of the traps that Satan is setting. He would love to see me stumble and fall. He wants to lure Your children away from You. Be my rock and my fortress. Protect me from his evil schemes. Be my refuge, I pray. Amen.

Since you are my rock and my fortress, for the sake of your name lead and guide me. Keep me free from the trap that is set for me, for you are my refuge.

PSALM 31:3–4 NIV

Day 280

Supernatural Peace

Lord, help untangle my emotions and sort my jumbled thoughts. Calm my restless spirit. Ease my anxieties. Help me experience Your supernatural peace in a real and tangible way. I know that true peace can come only from You, heavenly Father. Amen.

Then you will experience God's peace, which exceeds anything we can understand. His peace will guard your hearts and minds as you live in Christ Jesus.

PHILIPPIANS 4:7 NLT

Day 281

Gentle, Loving Hands

Heavenly Father, I long for Your peace in my heart. Please take every anxious thread, every tightly pulled knot of uncertainty, sorrow, conflict, and disappointment into Your gentle, loving hands. You are always enough for me. I am so thankful to be Your child. Amen.

"Are God's consolations not enough for you, words spoken gently to you?"

JOB 15:11 NIV

Delightful Little Gifts

Father, when happiness is hard to come by, help me to learn to draw more consistently on Your wellspring of joy. Help me delight in the little gifts You bring my way every day. I ask that You make me a notice of simple pleasures and I ask that You put bright spots in the days of those I love. We need to know that You are here with us. In Jesus' name I pray, amen.

One God

Lord, Your Word says that salvation is found in no one else but Jesus Christ. Our society likes to try to convince me that I can find life in other ways. I choose to believe in Jesus, not in other gods, not in other religious philosophies, not in materialism. Amen.

"You must not bow down to them or worship them, for I, the LORD your God, am a jealous God who will not tolerate your affection for any other gods."
EXODUS 20:5 NLT

Day 284

I Will Trust

God, I wake up with anxiety at times. I fear the future, and I want to slow down the hands of time. I remember when I used to live in peace. I had not a worry in the world. As life goes on, I have grown more fearful. Please calm my racing mind and whisper to me a calm assurance that You have everything under control. Thank You, Father. Amen.

When I am afraid, I put my trust in you.
In God, whose word I praise—
in God I trust and am not afraid.

PSALM 56:3–4 NIV

Day 285

Before I Speak

O God, help me think before I speak. Put words of kindness in my mouth that will build up others instead of destroying them. I desire to be virtuous. Amen.

And so blessing and cursing come pouring out of the same mouth. Surely, my brothers and sisters, this is not right! Does a spring of water bubble out with both fresh water and bitter water? Does a fig tree produce olives, or a grapevine produce figs? No, and you can't draw fresh water from a salty spring.

JAMES 3:10–12 NLT

Day 286

"Whom Shall I Fear?"

Lord, as a mother, I've often found myself afraid. Please help me to remember where my strength and salvation come from and to say with confidence, "Whom shall I fear? Of whom shall I be afraid?" If my God is with me, who can be against me? If my God is with my children, why would I fear? Amen.

Day 287

Daily Needs

Lord, if I trust You for my eternal salvation, why don't I trust You for my daily needs? Like the Israelites who gathered more manna than they needed, I worry about the future instead of trusting You. Instill in me a trust that You will meet each need as it arises. Amen.

Then the LORD said to Moses, "Look, I'm going to rain down food from heaven for you. Each day the people can go out and pick up as much food as they need for that day. I will test them in this to see whether or not they will follow my instructions."

EXODUS 16:4 NLT

Give Joyously

Father, don't let me feel social pressure when giving. No matter how much or how little I can give, help me to give joyously and with a cheerful heart. Amen.

You must each decide in your heart how much to give. And don't give reluctantly or in response to pressure. "For God loves a person who gives cheerfully."

2 CORINTHIANS 9:7 NLT

Day 289

Teach Me Your Ways, Lord

God, just as Joseph found favor with You in Pharoah's courts and was blessed by Your hand, I pray that I will find favor with You as well. May You be pleased with me and with my children. May we walk in Your ways and be blessed by Your hand all the days of our lives. Amen.

"If you are pleased with me, teach me your ways so I may know you and continue to find favor with you."

EXODUS 33:13 NIV

Harvest of Righteousness

- -

Lord, plant Your wisdom in me like seeds in the soil. Help me cultivate each one and follow Your ways. They are pure, peace-loving, considerate, submissive, full of mercy and good fruit, impartial, and sincere. May I be a person who sows in peace and raises a harvest of righteousness. Amen.

*Peacemakers who sow in peace reap
a harvest of righteousness.*

JAMES 3:18 NIV

Words of Peace and Comfort

Lord, the next time I am angry, guide me away from sin until I can speak words of peace and comfort once again. Give me the strategies I need in order to refrain from sinning when I am angry. I want to be kind even when I am frustrated. Amen.

*"I hope I continue to please you, sir,"
she replied. "You have comforted me
by speaking so kindly to me, even though
I am not one of your workers."*

RUTH 2:13 NLT

The Power to Set Things Right

Lord, when my family is treated unfairly or when someone judges me before knowing the whole story, I want to see justice done. Remind me to rely on You for that justice. Only You have the power to set things right once and for all. Amen.

"For I am ready to set things right, not in the distant future, but right now! I am ready to save Jerusalem and show my glory to Israel."

ISAIAH 46:13 NLT

God Can Heal Every Hurt

Father, my heart is breaking. I need to know that You are near and that You care. Gently remind me that You have the power to heal every hurt and help me make it through what I'm facing right now. I have been broken-hearted before and You healed me then. I pray that once again You will show mercy upon me and bring me back to a joyous life. Amen.

Day 294

Redeem Me

You are the Great Redeemer. You bring beauty from ashes. You take what was dead and make it alive. You use broken vessels. You can use even me. I am so thankful for the redemption You provide, O God. Continue to renew my heart and make it clean and pure that I might bring You glory and honor. In Jesus' name I pray, amen.

Into your hands I commit my spirit;
deliver me, LORD, my faithful God.

PSALM 31:5 NIV

Day 295

Beyond Words

Lord, thank You for asking Jesus to pay the high price for what I've done. The thought of His sacrifice and Your unending grace humbles me beyond words. "Thank You" will never be enough. Amen.

Dear friends, you always followed my instructions when I was with you. And now that I am away, it is even more important. Work hard to show the results of your salvation, obeying God with deep reverence and fear.

PHILIPPIANS 2:12 NLT

True Change of Heart

- -

Father, every day is a battle. I struggle between following You and choosing what feels right at the moment. I need Your wisdom and power to persevere toward a true change of heart and action. But most of all, I need Your forgiveness. Amen.

"Watch and pray so that you will not fall into temptation. The spirit is willing, but the flesh is weak."

MATTHEW 26:41 NIV

Angels

- -

Heavenly Father, the world is a frightening place. I look around and see endless opportunities for disaster and tragedy. And yet, I place my trust in Your promise to send Your angels to watch over and guard me. Thank You for Your protection. Amen.

"And he will send his angels with a loud trumpet call, and they will gather his elect from the four winds, from one end of the heavens to the other."

MATTHEW 24:31 NIV

Day 298

God's Protection

Lord, I know I can't hope to escape every
unpleasant circumstance in this world. Just
the same, I will trust in You, whatever comes.
Protect me in the way You see fit, in the way
that best advances Your purpose for my life.
If tragedy should strike, because I know that
I am not immune from it, please allow me to
use even that for Your glory. There are no
accidents with You, and You bring good from
all things. Amen.

Open My Eyes, Lord

Open my eyes and reveal to me what You want me to glean from Your Word. Before I begin to read Your holy scriptures, I want to ask You to teach me very personally from them. I know that You want me to sit at Your feet and learn from Your teachings. Thank You, Lord, for the Bible, which is my instruction manual for life. Amen.

*Open my eyes that I may see
wonderful things in your law.*

PSALM 119:18 NIV

Day 300

Take My Hand, Lord

Lord, when it comes to courage, I have none of my own. Without You, I would be filled with fear, terrified of a future I cannot see. Thank You for patiently taking my hand and helping me face my fears. Amen.

David also said to Solomon his son, "Be strong and courageous, and do the work. Do not be afraid or discouraged, for the LORD God, my God, is with you. He will not fail you or forsake you until all the work for the service of the temple of the LORD is finished."

1 CHRONICLES 28:20 NIV

Day 301

A Prayer from Charlotte Elliott's Heart

Just as I am, without one plea, But that Thy blood was shed for me, And that Thou bidst me come to Thee, O Lamb of God, I come, I come. Just as I am, and waiting not To rid my soul of one dark blot, To Thee whose blood can cleanse each spot, O Lamb of God, I come, I come. Just as I am, poor, wretched, blind; Sight, riches, healing of the mind, Yea, all I need in Thee to find, O Lamb of God, I come, I come. Just as I am, Thou wilt receive, Wilt welcome, pardon, cleanse, relieve; Because Thy promise I believe, O Lamb of God, I come, I come.

Cleanse Me

Father, on my worst days I feel totally unworthy.
But I know You have promised to cleanse me
from all unrighteousness, to wipe away my guilt
and make me whole if I confess my sins. Amen.

*"I will cleanse them from all the sin they
have committed against me and will forgive
all their sins of rebellion against me."*

JEREMIAH 33:8 NIV

Day 303

Abundant Wisdom

Lord, life seems overwhelming to me sometimes. Please give me the abundant wisdom
You've promised and help me to relax in the
knowledge that You will guide me. I take great
comfort in knowing that if I ask, You will give
me wisdom. I am asking, Father. Hear me as
I pray. Amen.

*If any of you lacks wisdom, you should ask
God, who gives generously to all without
finding fault, and it will be given to you.*

JAMES 1:5 NIV

A Great Blessing

Father, I know it is Your will for me to understand Your Word, and You've given me the Holy Spirit to guide me. Help me to take advantage of this great blessing. Amen.

"But when he, the Spirit of truth, comes, he will guide you into all the truth. He will not speak on his own; he will speak only what he hears, and he will tell you what is yet to come."

JOHN 16:13 NIV

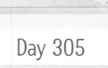

Day 305

Seasoned Speech

Lord, guard my tongue as I teach my children. Season my speech with grace—to encourage my children and remind them to walk in Your path. When my children have questions, I pray that You supply the answers, for on my own, I will have no words that will suffice. Thank You, Father, for hearing this prayer. Amen.

Let your conversation be always full of grace, seasoned with salt, so that you may know how to answer everyone.

COLOSSIANS 4:6 NIV

Teach Me, Lord

There is so much hustle and bustle all around me, Father. Help me to find quiet times even if I must rise much earlier or stay up later than my family. I need quiet time with You so that You can reveal truth to me. Examine my heart, Father God, and point out to me where I am wrong. I want to grow, and I know that this will involve discipline. Amen.

*"Teach me, and I will be quiet;
show me where I have been wrong."*

JOB 6:24 NIV

Day 307

Blessed Assurance

- -

Lord, there are many forces in the world that are coming against my children and me. Your Word says that there is nothing in heaven or on earth that can separate us from Your love. Thank You for Your wonderful reassurance. *Blessed assurance, Jesus is mine! Oh, what a foretaste of glory divine! Heir of salvation, purchase of God, born of His Spirit, washed in His blood.* Amen.

A Clear Understanding

- -

Lord, as I read and study Your Word and hear sermons preached about it, I still have questions and much to learn. I ask that You give me a clear understanding of what You are saying to me through it. Help me to take notes and to study the scriptures that the pastor references. I know that I can learn and grow spiritually as I do these things. Amen.

Day 309

Think, Then Speak

I'm ashamed to admit that I often speak before I think, and the words that come out of my mouth are anything but wise. Help my children to be wise enough to think first, then speak. Please help me be a good example. Amen.

This you know, my beloved brethren. But everyone must be quick to hear, slow to speak and slow to anger.

JAMES 1:19 NASB

Day 310

Good Judgment

You're a good Father and I am loved by You.
Grant me good judgment and teach me Your
ways. Amen.

Do good to your servant
according to your word, LORD.
Teach me knowledge and good judgment,
for I trust your commands.
Before I was afflicted I went astray,
but now I obey your word.
You are good, and what you do is good;
teach me your decrees.

PSALM 119:65–68 NIV

Day 311

An Overcomer

Lord, there are many times when I need You
and Your Word to guide me. Lead me and help
me become an overcomer. You tell me in Your
Word that I am more than a conqueror through
Jesus Christ, Your Son. Amen.

*No, in all these things we are more than
conquerors through him who loved us.*
ROMANS 8:37 NIV

The Covering of Jesus' Blood

There is no condemnation for us when we believe in You, Jesus. The covering of Your blood helps us to prevail over anything. We never need to fear anymore. Thank You for giving us this victory. My sins are washed away because You died for me. *What can wash away my sin? Nothing but the blood of Jesus; What can make me whole again? Nothing but the blood of Jesus. Oh! precious is the flow that makes me white as snow; No other fount I know, Nothing but the blood of Jesus.* Amen.

Day 313

Press On

- -

Lord, help me to forget the things in my past that I need to leave behind. Give me courage to press on. There is a reward in heaven—and I want to win the prize! Help me to face forward and march boldly into the future. Amen.

Brothers and sisters, I do not consider myself yet to have taken hold of it. But one thing I do: Forgetting what is behind and straining toward what is ahead, I press on toward the goal to win the prize for which God has called me heavenward in Christ Jesus.

PHILIPPIANS 3:13–14 NIV

Day 314

Prayer for Society

Lord, the fabric of our society has been unraveling for some time. May healing begin as those of us who believe in You call upon Your name, seek Your face, and turn from our own wicked ways—so You will hear from heaven, forgive our sins, and heal our land. Amen.

"If my people, who are called by my name, will humble themselves and pray and seek my face and turn from their wicked ways, then I will hear from heaven, and I will forgive their sin and will heal their land."

2 CHRONICLES 7:14 NIV

Day 315

Worship in Harmony

Lord, I pray for each member of this church—
that we would get along. Despite our variety of
backgrounds and opinions, help us to live and
worship in harmony. Give us the ability to value
and respect our differences. Protect us against
divisions, and help us to be like-minded. Amen.

Then the church throughout Judea,
Galilee and Samaria enjoyed a time of
peace and was strengthened. Living in
the fear of the Lord and encouraged by
the Holy Spirit, it increased in numbers.

ACTS 9:31 NIV

Day 316

Never Abandon Hope

When all hope seems lost, Lord, be with those who suffer. Be with those who are just about to give up today. Renew their minds. Help them never to abandon hope, for all things are possible with You. You are the hope of believers all around the world in all types of circumstances. Amen.

"You will be secure, because there is hope; you will look about you and take your rest in safety."

JOB 11:18 NIV

My Longings and My Purpose

Lord, help me hold on to hope. Abraham had great faith in You and became the father of many nations. Though he was old, You provided a son for him and his wife, Sarah. As You did for them, please fulfill my longings—and Your vision for my life's purpose. Amen.

Abraham fell facedown; he laughed and said to himself, "Will a son be born to a man a hundred years old? Will Sarah bear a child at the age of ninety?"

GENESIS 17:17 NIV

Day 318

Prayer for Healing

Lord, I have prayed, and healing hasn't come.
It's hard to know why You do not heal when
You clearly have the power to do so. Please
help me not to focus on my present suffering,
but to be transformed in my attitude. I know
that You will heal me either here on earth or
in heaven one day when You give me a new
body. Help me to trust that You know what is
best for me. Amen.

Day 319

The Righteous Are Blessed

Sometimes, Father, I sense Your protection and Your blessing. I find favor with my employer or someone in authority over me. I sense that You are in that, God. I have a near-miss on the interstate that could have turned into a horrible wreck. I know that Your angels protected me. God, I pray that You will continue to surround me with Your favor. I need You every day, every hour, every moment. Amen.

Surely, LORD, you bless the righteous;
you surround them with your
favor as with a shield.
PSALM 5:12 NIV

Day 320

Weakness into Strength

Lord, show me all the good You have done for the faithful throughout history, and give me some of Your strength when my own fails. Let my dependence on You turn weakness into strength. Amen.

But he said to me, "My grace is sufficient for you, for my power is made perfect in weakness." Therefore I will boast all the more gladly about my weaknesses, so that Christ's power may rest on me.

2 CORINTHIANS 12:9 NIV

Day 321

Praying for Leaders

Lord, may our city leaders lead with integrity, honesty, and fairness. Help the people I pray for now to lead with justice, grace, and mercy: the mayor, our judges and court officials, members of the police and fire departments, and other civic leaders. Amen.

Remind the people to be subject to rulers and authorities, to be obedient, to be ready to do whatever is good, to slander no one, to be peaceable and considerate, and always to be gentle toward everyone.

TITUS 3:1–2 NIV

Day 322

Rescued

Lord, Your love is so strong that You swept down to snatch me from the gravest times of my life. You know how hard things have been; I thought I was going to die. But I didn't. And it's all because of Your power of deliverance. I praise You, Lord! Help me to live out the rest of my days as a godly woman who testifies of Your goodness and saving grace. Amen.

Day 323

Eternal Care

Father, my trials are not major, so far. But I know that things can go wrong in an instant. When I cry to You, I know You hear. Thank You for Your promises and Your never-ending care. I know that I should consider even my trials pure joy, for You are with me, molding my character through them. Amen.

Consider it pure joy, my brothers and sisters, whenever you face trials of many kinds.

JAMES 1:2 NIV

Day 324

Righteous Judgment

Help me, God, not to seek revenge. When someone hurts me, I know that You see the pain. You have forgiven me, and I know that I should not wish bad things upon someone just because they disappointed me or wounded me in some way. Help me to leave the judgment to You, trusting that You will make all things right one day. Amen.

My enemies turn back; they stumble and perish before you. For you have upheld my right and my cause, sitting enthroned as the righteous judge.

PSALM 9:3–4 NIV

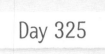

I Know He Loves Me

- -

Father, I pray You will always be my Rock, my salvation. Hear me when I call to You for help, for I know You love me. Amen.

Respect and Affection

Father, when I hear myself belittle my husband or speak to him harshly, remind me that Your standard for marriage is common respect and affection. I have found this man with Your help, and I love him. Help me to show him that every day and to affirm him rather than seeking to tear him down. I want to honor You in my marriage even on days when this is not an easy task. Amen.

Firm Yet Tender

- -

Lord, give me wisdom and strength in my instruction to my children. Help me to be firm
when I need to be, yet tender and giving as
the teaching allows. Guide me in how to show
love for You and Your laws. Amen.

*Discipline your children, for in
that there is hope; do not be a
willing party to their death.*

PROVERBS 19:18 NIV

Day 328

Never-Ending Blessings

Heavenly Father, I have so much to be thankful for. My list of blessings is never ending. May I never fail to praise You and to thank You for the many blessings You have given to me. Amen.

How abundant are the good things that you have stored up for those who fear you, that you bestow in the sight of all, on those who take refuge in you.

PSALM 31:19 NIV

Day 329

Wonders of God

Blessed is the one who trusts in the LORD,
who does not look to the proud,
to those who turn aside to false gods.
Many, LORD my God, are the wonders you
have done, the things you planned for us.
None can compare with you;
were I to speak and tell of your deeds,
they would be too many to declare.
Sacrifice and offering you did not desire—
but my ears you have opened—burnt
offerings and sin offerings you did not require.
Then I said, "Here I am, I have come—
it is written about me in the scroll.
I desire to do your will, my God;
your law is within my heart."

PSALM 40:4–8 NIV

A Prayer from Catherine of Genoa's Heart

I do not want to turn my eyes from You, O God. There I want them to stay and not move no matter what happens to me, within or without. For those who trust in God need not worry about themselves. As I think about you, my spiritual children, I see that God's pure love is attentive to all your needs. It is because of His tender love I need not ask anything of God for you. All I need to do is lift you up before His face.

Turning from Sin

- -

Father, help me show my children the need for
self-control, not to give in to the temptation of
sin. Only when we turn from sin can we truly
gain understanding in all wisdom. We ask for
Your strength to help in this. Amen.

*"Therefore, you Israelites, I will judge
each of you according to your own ways,
declares the Sovereign LORD. Repent!
Turn away from all your offenses;
then sin will not be your downfall."*

EZEKIEL 18:30 NIV

Day 332

Like You, Jesus

Lord, fill me with compassion for my fellow Christians so I might be a godly example of love and understanding. I want to emulate You, Jesus. Amen.

God is love. Whoever lives in love lives in God, and God in them. This is how love is made complete among us so that we will have confidence on the day of judgment: In this world we are like Jesus. There is no fear in love. But perfect love drives out fear, because fear has to do with punishment. The one who fears is not made perfect in love.

1 JOHN 4:16–18 NIV

Day 333

A Continuous Desire

Father, help me to be diligent in understanding You and Your precepts. Please give me a continuous desire to know You better and to become more like You. You have called me to good works so that others may see a difference in me and glorify my Father, who is in heaven. Amen.

For God called you to do good, even if it means suffering, just as Christ suffered for you. He is your example, and you must follow in his steps.

1 PETER 2:21 NLT

Explanation of Peace

Lord, I explained peace to my children today as being a core of calm deep inside. No matter what happens to upset us on the surface, You are in our innermost being, bringing peace and comfort. Thank You that we can always trust You, even in the midst of life's greatest storms. Amen.

You rule the oceans.
You subdue their storm-tossed waves.

PSALM 89:9 NLT

Lead Me to the Rock

God, I am so weary. I have been through so much. Where are You? Are You able to hear my cries? Day after day, I agonize. I am anxious about the future. I call out to You. Father, set my feet on solid ground. You are the Rock of my salvation. I know that I can stand if You stand with me. Amen.

From the ends of the earth I call to you,
I call as my heart grows faint; lead me
to the rock that is higher than I.

PSALM 61:2 NIV

Day 336

Like a Tree

Lord, I feel like a withered plant with dry, brown leaves. Help me connect with You in prayer so I can grow strong and healthy like a vibrant green tree. You are my Source of living water. Amen.

Oh, the joys of those who do not follow the advice of the wicked, or stand around with sinners, or join in with mockers. But they delight in the law of the LORD, meditating on it day and night. They are like trees planted along the riverbank, bearing fruit each season. Their leaves never wither, and they prosper in all they do.

PSALM 1:1–3 NLT

A Way of Escape

There are days when I don't know how much longer I can go on. But Your Word says that You will provide a way of escape. You help us overcome our temptations. Thank You for Your promise. Amen.

If you think you are standing strong, be careful not to fall. The temptations in your life are no different from what others experience. And God is faithful. He will not allow the temptation to be more than you can stand. When you are tempted, he will show you a way out so that you can endure.

1 CORINTHIANS 10:12–13 NLT

Protection

Father, many temptations come from evil forces that are so deceptive they are hard to see. The devil fights against us daily. Thank You for providing a way that we can be protected from the full assault of Satan's deceitfulness. Amen.

The sinful nature wants to do evil, which is just the opposite of what the Spirit wants. And the Spirit gives us desires that are the opposite of what the sinful nature desires. These two forces are constantly fighting each other, so you are not free to carry out your good intentions.

GALATIANS 5:17 NLT

Day 339

Fill Me, Lord

Lord, I am weary. Infuse me with life, energy, and joy again. I don't have to look to a bowl of ice cream or the compliments of a friend to fill me up on the inside. Steady and constant, You are the One who fills me. Amen.

Oh, how generous and gracious our Lord was! He filled me with the faith and love that come from Christ Jesus.

1 TIMOTHY 1:14 NLT

Day 340

Sheep of His Pasture

Thank You, Lord, for Your love and faithfulness to us. Thank You for making us Your people and for allowing us to be the sheep of Your pasture. Thank You for allowing us to serve such a great God! I will teach Your ways to my children. It is my deep desire as a mother that our family will praise Your name from generation to generation. Amen.

Then we your people, the sheep of your pasture, will thank you forever and ever, praising your greatness from generation to generation.

PSALM 79:13 NLT

Everlasting

- -

Father God, the heroes my children admire today have weaknesses. They are actors or actresses, singers and such. They are human, and many of them are not following after You. But not You, Lord; You are perfect. Your strength is everlasting. Help my children to trust You as their only hero—the One they can trust forever and ever. You are greater than any other, and You will always come through for us. Amen.

Day 342

Omnipotent

I know I can trust in You, Lord. Thank You for Your strength, which never fails. It is there for all eternity. You don't weaken like I do. You are omnipotent. All honor goes to the One who is everlasting. You alone are God. Amen.

All honor and glory to God forever and ever! He is the eternal King, the unseen one who never dies; he alone is God. Amen.

1 TIMOTHY 1:17 NLT

Day 343

Firmly Planted

- -

Lord, as my children grow, help me to treat them like young trees, planting them firmly in Your Word. Then, as I see them getting stronger every day, I pray that they will trust You and be blessed. I pray that they will bear much fruit for Your kingdom. Amen.

They are like trees planted along the riverbank, bearing fruit each season. Their leaves never wither, and they prosper in all they do.

PSALM 1:3 NLT

Day 344

Self-Control

- -

Lord, please create in me the fruit of self-control. Empower me to walk in Your Spirit's power and to flee temptation. Help me to change the channel or to walk away from the food or to put my credit cards out of reach when I've been using them too much. Help me to think before I act. I know that my life will benefit greatly if I am able to increase my self-control. Amen.

*A person without self-control is like
a city with broken-down walls.*

PROVERBS 25:28 NLT

Day 345

Keep Me Anchored

Lord, I want my heart to continually be filled with praise and thanksgiving to You. Keep me anchored in the thought that all You do is for my good and glory. Make my heart steadfast and keep me from temptation. Only You are deserving of my praise and adoration. Amen.

Evil people try to drag me into sin, but I am firmly anchored to your instructions.

Psalm 119:61 NLT

Day 346

Best Friend

Lord, I hear others speak of their BFFs. They post pictures on social media sites and it used to make me feel left out. Not anymore! Lord, You are my best friend. How could it be anyone else! You are kind, loving, generous, faithful, and giving. You always listen, and You always care. And You have the best advice. But most of all, You laid down Your life for me—for *me*, Lord! Amen.

"Greater love has no one than this,
that one lay down his life for his friends."

JOHN 15:13 NASB

Wise Choices

Lord, help me to order my days so my priorities reflect Yours—so that I spend my time and energy as You would want me to. Amid the activity bombarding my life, center me on You. Teach me Christ-centered living so that wise choices will follow. Amen.

"Is not wisdom found among the aged?
Does not long life bring understanding?"

JOB 12:12 NIV

Day 348

All Glory

Lord, I pray that my children and their children and each successive generation will understand that all the glory for our many blessings belongs to You. Without You we would be nothing and would have nothing. May we praise Your name throughout the generations! Amen.

To him be glory in the church and in Christ Jesus throughout all generations, for ever and ever! Amen.

EPHESIANS 3:21 NIV

Day 349

Eternal God

- -

Alpha and Omega, Beginning and End, from everlasting to everlasting You are God. In the beginning was the Word and the Word was with God and the Word was God. It is all a mystery that will be made clear one day. For now, I rest in the assurance that my God is really big. You are the Great I Am, Jesus, Redeemer, and Friend. I will trust in You. Amen.

Lord, you have been our dwelling place throughout all generations. Before the mountains were born or you brought forth the whole world, from everlasting to everlasting you are God.

PSALM 90:1–2 NIV

Day 350

Sufficient Strength

Father, I praise You for Your support. When my strength fails, Yours is always sufficient. Thank You for Your constant love and care, for knowing me by name, picking out my cry in the night, and never failing to rescue me. Amen.

"The gatekeeper opens the gate for him, and the sheep recognize his voice and come to him. He calls his own sheep by name and leads them out."

JOHN 10:3 NLT

Accepting God's Promises

Lord, help me to remember that although Your promises are free for the taking, I still need to accept them, claim them, and then live in faith that they are mine. Amen.

Communication with My Husband

Lord, I thank You for my wonderful husband. I truly love him, but I need more; I need better communication with him. Help me not to fear asking for what I need emotionally. I pray that You would speak to his heart, and that he would learn to listen. Amen.

In the same way, husbands ought to love their wives as they love their own bodies. For a man who loves his wife actually shows love for himself.

EPHESIANS 5:28 NLT

Day 353

A Fruitful Vine

I want to be a fruitful vine, Lord. With Your help I can, whether the fruit I bring is a cheerful attitude or money to help provide for my family. Show me the best way to contribute to the happiness of my home and family. Amen.

"He cuts off every branch of mine that doesn't produce fruit, and he prunes the branches that do bear fruit so they will produce even more."

JOHN 15:2 NLT

Day 354

Those in Prison

Lord, I bring before You those who are in prison. Help them to know that only You offer a life of hope and peace. In the darkness, help them to find Christ's forgiveness, joy, and light. Remind me to visit those in prison and fulfill Your commands. Amen.

Remember those in prison, as if you were there yourself. Remember also those being mistreated, as if you felt their pain in your own bodies.

HEBREWS 13:3 NLT

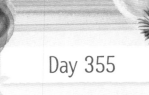

Boundaries

Thank You, Father, for giving us sound doctrine.
I have boundaries set by You that I can follow
and teach to my children. All we have to do is
look to You and Your Word for guidance. The
boundaries You have established for me have
fallen in pleasant places. Amen.

*The boundary lines have fallen for
me in pleasant places; surely I
have a delightful inheritance.*

PSALM 16:6 NIV

Day 356

Promise of Protection

Please protect my children, Lord. I've tried to
instill godly values, but I can't be with them all
the time. Please send Your Spirit with them.
Keep them from being corrupted and led away
from Your truth. Amen.

*He will cover you with his feathers, and
under his wings you will find refuge; his
faithfulness will be your shield and rampart.*

PSALM 91:4 NIV

Day 357

New in Christ

Father, thanks to You I get to start over, fresh and clean, because You have made me a new person. I am forgiven and free in Christ Jesus. I now have a lifetime of new days to spend any way I choose. Help me to spend each day bringing glory to You in some way. I am so amazed that I have a clean slate to fill with good things. Thank You for Your never-ending forgiveness. Amen.

Deliverance

Lord, I need deliverance from my anxiety. I am not responsible for everyone and everything—You are, and I know You are trustworthy. Why do I toss and turn in my bed, analyzing and pondering every little issue? I want to surrender my worries to You. Help me to hope in You and trust Your protection. I ask this in the powerful, healing name of Jesus. Amen.

When anxiety was great within me,
your consolation brought me joy.

PSALM 94:19 NIV

Day 359

Workplace Relationships

- -

Lord, I thank You for my coworkers. Even
though we're all busy, help us to have more
connectedness and unity so we can be more
efficient and find more enjoyment in our work.
Please bless my relationships in the workplace.
Help me to put others above myself. Help us
to work well as a team, I pray. Amen.

*Not looking to your own interests but each
of you to the interests of the others.*

PHILIPPIANS 2:4 NIV

A Prayer from Fanny J. Crosby's Heart

Blessed assurance, Jesus is mine! O what a foretaste of glory divine! Heir of salvation, purchase of God, born of his Spirit, washed in his blood. This is my story, this is my song, praising my Savior all the day long; this is my story, this is my song, praising my Savior all the day long.

Day 361

Comfort My Friend

Lord, my friend has deep pain in her soul. I ask that You would comfort her. May she rest in the strong and loving arms of the One who loves her most. Heal her heartache, heal her sorrow. You are acquainted with grief, so You know her pain. Amen.

He was despised and forsaken of men, a man of sorrows and acquainted with grief; and like one from whom men hide their face He was despised, and we did not esteem Him.

ISAIAH 53:3 NASB

Day 362

Spiritual Gifts

Lord, help us to use our spiritual gifts, those talents and abilities You've given us, to serve in the church and in ministries. We are many, but we form one body. We have different gifts, according to what You've given, but we serve each other. Amen.

For just as each of us has one body with many members, and these members do not all have the same function, so in Christ we, though many, form one body, and each member belongs to all the others. We have different gifts, according to the grace given to each of us.

ROMANS 12:4–6 NIV

Day 363

God's Will

Father, I long to be a mother. If it is Your will, there will be children. If this is not the path You have chosen for me, I trust in You and know You will make my life meaningful in other ways. Amen.

In her deep anguish Hannah prayed to the LORD, weeping bitterly. And she made a vow, saying, "LORD Almighty, if you will only look on your servant's misery and remember me, and not forget your servant but give her a son, then I will give him to the LORD for all the days of his life."

1 SAMUEL 1:10–11 NIV

Day 364

Heal and Save Me

Lord, I choose to praise You through this pain. You are great, and there is no one worthy of Your honor and glory. "Heal me, LORD, and I will be healed; save me and I will be saved, for you are the one I praise" (Jeremiah 17:14 NIV). Amen.

And hearing this, Jesus said to them, "It is not those who are healthy who need a physician, but those who are sick; I did not come to call the righteous, but sinners."

MARK 2:17 NASB

Day 365

A New Name

Thank You, Father God, that You reached down and saved me from myself. I was on the road to nowhere. Just as You did with Saul, You made Yourself known to me at just the right time. You have given me a new name. I am a child of the Living God. I thank You, Father, for casting my sin away as far as the east is from the west and remembering it no more! Amen.

Do not remember the sins of my youth and my rebellious ways; according to your love remember me, for you, LORD, are good.

PSALM 25:7 NIV

Scripture Index

Proverbs

Isaiah

Jeremiah

Everyday Prayers for Your Heart

Envelop your spirit in the comfort of the
heavenly Father with these heartfelt prayers
and encouraging scriptures.

I will give thanks to you, LORD, with all my heart;
I will tell of all your wonderful deeds.
I will be glad and rejoice in you;
I will sing the praises of your name, O Most High.

PSALM 9:1–2 NIV

Religion / Christian Life / Prayer

U.S. $9.99

ISBN 978-1-64352-968-4

50999

BARBOUR
PUBLISHING